Timber Preservation Guide

Revised 2020

Edgar Stubbersfield

Copyright © 2012, 2020 Rachel Stubbersfield
All rights reserved.
ISBN13: 978-0-6486781-2-0

DEDICATION

This guide to timber preservation is dedicated Henri Bailleres, an original thinker and a great problem solver when it comes to the issues of timber. I am honored to be his friend. Henri has been a great encouragement to me in my writing.

CONTENTS

	Acknowledgments	Pg i
	Abbreviations	Pg ii
	About the Author	Pg 1
	Introduction	Pg 2
1	Preliminary Matters	Pg 3
2	Hazard Levels and Timber	Pg 7
3	Common Treatment Options	Pg 10
4	Effectiveness of Treating	Pg 21
5	Branding and Identification	Pg 34
6	Preservation and Corrosion	Pg 37
7	Preservation and Colour	Pg 50
8	When is a preservative not a Preservative	Pg 55
9	Special considerations with CCA	Pg 57
10	Preservation Warranties	Pg 63
11	Sampling and Testing	Pg 64
12	Some Preservation Case Histories	Pg 67
	Conclusion	Pg 73
	Source of Images	Pg 74
	References	Pg 75

ACKNOWLEDGMENTS

This Guide started life as a series in my 2010 newsletters for Outdoor Structures Australia. When I started writing the expanded document, I had no idea how far I would proceed as it needed the assistance of many people to come to completion. I was surprised at how helpful people would prove to be and wish to acknowledge the encouragement they have been. If this Guide proves to be of service to you, it is in no small part because of these people.

Greg Jensen
Commercial and Regulatory Manager, Lonza Wood Protection

Steven Koch
Business Development Manage, Lonza Wood Protection

Dan Tingley
Senior Structural Engineer, Wood Technologist
Wood Research and Development, Corvallis, Oregon

Afzal Laphir
Engineering Manager, Pryda Australia

Dr Harry Greaves BTech, DIC, PhD, DSc
Principal, HG Consulting

Doug Howick FIWSc
Secretary, Timber Preservers Association of Australia

While this book does not claim to represent the views of the Department of Agriculture, Fisheries. The assistance of three of its officers is especially acknowledged.

Gary Hopewell AD AppSc (Forestry), MSc (WoodSc)
Senior Technician, Forest Product Innovations, Agri-Science Queensland

Jack Norton B App Sc (Chem.), Grad Dip Bus. Admin, Grad Dip Comp.Sc., M Tech Mngt, M Phil Chem Eng,,
Formerly *Leader Product Performance,* Agri-Science Queensland

William Leggate Team Leader and Principal Research Scientist, Forest Products Innovation
Agri-Science Queensland

The assistance of ENERGEX is also appreciated.
Finally, Dennis and Carol Clark, for their years of friendship and photography,

ABBREVIATIONS

ACQ	Ammonia Copper Quaternary
AGD	Above ground durability
APAS	Australian Paint Approval Scheme
APVMA	Australian Pesticides and Veterinary Medicines Authority
BaP	Benzo-α-pryene
BCA	Building Code of Australia
CCA	Copper chrome arsenic
CBA	Copper boron azole
CN	Copper naphthenate
CSIRO	Commonwealth Scientific & Industrial Research Organisation
CTIQ	Construction Timbers in Queensland
EP	Electroplated
HDG	Hot dipped galvanised
IGD	In ground durability
LOSP	Light Organic Solvent Preservative
LVL	Laminated Veneer Lumber
NZBC	New Zealand Building Code
OSA	Outdoor Structures Australia
PCP	Pentachlorophenol
PEC	Pigment emulsified creosote
SS	Stainless steel
SUSDP	Standard for the Uniform Scheduling of Drugs and Poisons
TBTO	Tributyltin oxide
TBTN	Tributyltin naphthenate
TMA	Timber Marketing Act
TPAA	Timber Preservers Association of Australia
TUMA	Timber Utilisation and Marketing Act
TUPA	Timber Users Protection Act

ABOUT THE AUTHOR

Ted Stubbersfield was born in the small Queensland town of Gatton in 1950. After studying to be a pastor in Brisbane and the UK he returned to the family business, Gatton Sawmilling Co. A fair question would be, can anything good come out of Gatton? Well, Gatton was the home of a Governor General of Australia (William Vanneck 1938). It is also the home of the best and most innovative hardwood producer in Australia, Outdoor Structures Australia (OSA).

The family had been involved in sawmilling and building for about 140 years and a lot of knowledge has passed through the generations. In 1985 we ventured into the footbridge market (almost by accident) and then followed public landscaping. Initially we just did as we were told by consultants who knew very little about timber. In about 1988 Ted decided he would come to know the medium he was working with far better than any of his competitors and most of the professionals who used his products.

Ted realised that there were no useful standards and guides for designing and building weather exposed timber structures such as boardwalks. That led in 1997 to his first formal research project on boardwalk design, engineering supply and construction. Over the years there followed a complete set of guides. These allowed professionals to design timber structures of exceptional beauty and durability. Typically, everybody wants to re-invent the wheel and the guides were usually ignored. Invariably, the same mistakes keep being made over and over. This little book is an attempt to remedy this.

In 2012, the time came to close the manufacturing arm of OSA and to take on a less stressful lifestyle. Ted plans to put in writing much of what he has learnt so the industry does not have to relearn it. This book is the first in a series of Timber Design Files that are intended to allow designers to avoid the pitfalls of common but often bad practice and Standards that can be very inadequate and engender a false sense of security.

INTRODUCTION

A very senior engineer at a leading firm of consultants in Brisbane told me about his ability to very quickly home in on the mistakes of the junior engineers fresh out of university. Apparently, they are amazed at this uncanny ability until he breaks the truth to them. Instead of this being some superhuman skill, he had simply made exactly the same mistakes when he was young. When it comes to timber preservation, I think I have made my fair share of mistakes too. I shudder at some of the ill-informed advice I gave in my early days in the timber industry. Sadly, it was usually the normal advice everyone gave. This booklet is intended to guide professional designers through a maze of complex issues and so avoid mistakes I and others have made.

The main emphasis of this brief guide is to understand the issues relating to treatment in weather exposed applications. This guide will briefly look at some theory relating to timber treatment and show the requirements of *AS1604.1 Specification for preservative treatment, Part 1: Sawn and round timber*. This is followed by a more detailed look at practical matters associated with treatment and includes discussion about whether much of the Standard that specifiers rely on can actually be achieved. My concern has been that the designer is left with a sense of false security as, on many occasions, "preservation" of sawn timber simply has not been achieved.

This Guide concludes with case histories where what is learnt about preservation and natural durability throughout the following pages is applied to difficult durability applications.

The first edition of this book was written when the 2010 version of AS 1604.1 was current. The contents were reviewed in July 2015 as I had access to extra images and information about warranties had changed. As well the book was checked to ensure that any changes to AS 1604.1 – 2012 were incorporated. This standard upgrade mainly addressed the extra uses of Azole treatment and the introduction of H2F a lighter internal treatment for pine in areas where the great northern termite was not active. This 2020 edition was also needed to comment on:

- Increased use of spraying and dipping
- Increased use of glueline preservatives in engineered wood
- Codemarked timber selling alongside of Australian Standard timber
- Need for documentation of treated timber; and,
- Recognition of the need to do due diligence when purchasing

While AS1604.1 is the main emphasis of this guide, reference will be made to other standards in the series such as AS1604.2, 3, 4 and 5 which relate to reconstituted wood products, plywood, laminated veneer lumber (LVL) and laminated beams respectively. The draft standard from 2018 has also been considered The Increased use of modified wood is not covered in this edition.

Disclaimer
The information shown herein does not constitute a complete design so a Consulting Engineer with skills in both timber design and foundation systems should be engaged for the structural and foundation design.

1 PRELIMINARY MATTERS

The Importance of Timber Preservation

It must be accepted that wood is perishable; timber may suffer deterioration through the action of insects, fungi and marine boring organisms. This deterioration, however, can be reduced if conditions are made unsuitable for these destructive agents. Timber preservation changes the natural durability of the sapwood, rendering it toxic and thus unpalatable to insects, fungi and marine borers. Many timber species proved to be highly durable and have provided long service before the widespread introduction of the timber treatment industry. De-sapped In-Ground Durability 1 "bush poles" provided the power authorities with a life of fifty years or more.[1] Unfortunately, now there is not enough of the most durable timber available to meet the requirements. Preservation allows a much wider range of species to be utilised, even the least durable. (e.g. pine)

Even when dealing with the most durable timbers it has been found that the sapwood is always non-durable and will rapidly deteriorate if not protected. For example, the sapwood of ironbark should be considered no more durable than the sapwood of pine. So, the timber preservation industry provides the dual role of making non-durable timbers durable and preserving the sapwood of durable and non-durable species.

With the declining availability of high durability hardwoods, compounded by the disinclination by builders to use them due to their cost and weight, preservation of non-durable timbers is critical.

The Importance of Good Design

Timber treatment is not a substitute for good design; rather it is its handmaiden. Australian engineers and architects generally enter their profession with a sound knowledge of steel and concrete but have very little formal training in timber. While they have a good understanding of the science involved in calculating member and fastener sizes, most have little understanding of the art of timber design. It is an art, and some have jokingly referred to it as a dark art. Generally, I encounter drawings for projects that are designed for strength, and unquestionably are mathematically correct, but most are not designed for durability. Examples of durability problems that can be avoided at the design stage are narrow joists that split due to fastener damage, joints that hold moisture and specifying low grade and/or non-durable timbers. No amount of treating will overcome these design shortcomings.

Figure 1. Diagonal crossarm system invented by the author

An example of the primacy of design over treatment is taken from a problematic power line at the back of Mullumbimby in NSW where our crossarm mounting system was trialled (Figure 1). We had developed and patented a system of mounting crossarms on powerpoles that rotated the arm 45 degrees, so the moisture ran off. An extra benefit was that often the top of the arm was partly shaded during the day. The control arms were incised, pigment emulsified creosote (PEC) treated tallowwood, mounted in the normal manner and our arms were sap free untreated hardwood to one of the species in their specification. They were mounted on the same pole. After 3 years some of the control arms were being replaced whereas there wasn't even any mould growth on our arms!

---

[1] Leightley, L.E. Technical and Operational Aspects and In-Service Performance of Preservative Treated Poles in *Proceedings of the ESAA Pole Symposium,* Gold Coast, 1980.

As a footnote, we never sold any of these crossarm systems. They were a little more expensive, but only a little more and nothing in comparison with replacement costs. One authority did say that they never wanted to be locked into a situation where they could only purchase from one supplier. Outdated design practices continued and some timber crossarms continued underperforming. In a short period, I expect that this will be another market, ideally suited to timber because of its lack of conductivity, completely lost to substitutes such as fibre composites. Improved design would have seen this industry continue.

Natural Durability

Invariably, successful use of timber in challenging conditions is a combination of artificial durability achieved through added chemicals and the timbers own natural durability. The heartwood of all timbers can be classified according to its natural durability (or resistance) against attack by wood destroying organisms such as termites, borers and decay fungi. The resistance is due to the presence of special tannins, oils, resins and extractives in the heartwood that repel or kill insects and decay fungi. Examples of each (in ground) are shown below.

Note: Natural durability only refers to the mature outer heartwood. Sapwood of all timber species should be considered as being non-durable.		
Class 1 (in ground)	Timber of the highest natural durability which may be expected to resist decay for at least 25 years and up to 50 years	grey box grey ironbark red ironbark yellow box yellow gum tallowwood
Class 2 (in ground)	Timbers of high natural durability that may be expected to have a life of 15 to 25 years	jarrah river red gum white mahogany yellow stringybark red box spotted gum white cypress pine western red cedar
Class 3 (in ground)	Timbers of moderate durability that may be expected to last about 8 to 15 years	broad leaved peppermint southern blue gum Sydney blue gum brush box manna gum candle bark
Class 4 (in ground)	Timbers of low durability that may be expected to last from 1 to 8 years. These timbers have about the same durability as untreated sapwood which is generally regarded as class 4 regardless of species	mountain ash Douglas fir (Oregon) radiata pine hoop pine slash pine
Table 1. Natural In Ground Durability ratings		

A common mistake when referring to reference documents is not appreciating that the published durability level refers only to the heartwood. The sapwood when untreated is always **In Ground** or **Above Ground Durability 4** depending on the application. Some timbers have broad sapwood band so a large portion of a sawn member can be Durability 4 despite the heart being for example, Durability 2 as in white cypress shown in Figure 2. We have found this distinction to be a particular problem with this species where timber with low durability sapwood is used for decking.

Figure 2. The sapwood band varies from slight to major on these white cypress pine logs.

White cypress also brings up another important consideration. Its heartwood formerly used to be classed as Durability 1 In Ground and is now a Class 2 In Ground. It did not drop its durability say 25% overnight. It was borderline between the two and remains borderline. Similarly, a Durability 2 in ground species could be borderline to be a three. Knowing the real performance characteristics of the species being specified is very important in weather exposed situations.[2]

The Law and Standards

In 1987, the Queensland Government introduced the Timber Utilisation and Marketing Act (TUMA), an Act, which, among other matters, controlled the licensing and operation of treatment plants in that state. A radical innovation in the Queensland Act at the time was the introduction of Hazard or "H" levels. The Act, or more correctly its regulations, nominated six distinct levels of risk from decay and insect attack. These were easy to identify and easy to specify. This innovation was quickly adopted by AS1604.1 *Specification for preservative treatment* and now is becoming the standard designation of treatments worldwide, albeit with different terminology. The integrity of the treatment process in Queensland was initially ensured by a very rigorous system of plant registration, testing and reporting by Forestry Department inspectors.[3] Unfortunately, this Act was repealed in 2010. The Queensland Act was similar to the Timber Marketing Act 1977 (TMA) in New South Wales which was repealed in 2013. The reasons given for recalling the Queensland Act were firstly that there had been very few, if any, successful prosecutions under it but, despite that, it did serve as a break against flagrant abuses and established very clear goalposts. Another reason was that the Act, that had become lockstep with Australian Standards, was claimed to stifle innovation. A still further reason, its perceived redundancy following the introduction of the Australian Consumer Law in January 2011 and is discussed in the chapter, Preservation warranties.

There are a limited number of Australian Standards, such as *AS1684.2 Residential timber framed construction - Non-cyclonic areas*, *AS1720.1 Timber structures - Design methods* and *AS1720.5 Timber Structures – Timber properties* which are mentioned as primary references in National Construction Code[4] (formerly known as the Building Code of Australia or BCA). Other commonly used Standards in the timber industry such as AS1604.1 and the grading standards AS2082 and AS2858 are secondary references that get applied through being referenced in the primary or secondary standard. The

---

[2] An excellent source of information is *The In-ground Natural Durability of Australian Timbers* published by the Forest and Wood Products Research and Development Corporation and available at https://www.fwpa.com.au/images/marketaccess/PN04.1004.pdf
[3] This practice stopped around 2002-3.
[4] Found in Section B1.4 of Volume 1 of the 2019 edition.

compliance with these standards meets the *Deemed to Satisfy* requirement of the code. With repeal of the Acts, the authority of AS1604.1 was not diminished but any form of oversight was lost, in at least those two states. The other states simply never had any oversight at all. Having been involved in a long and expensive court battle over the resale of some Oregon rafters prior to the incorporation of the normal Standards that are used by the industry into the NCC, we argued that we supplied to the Australian Standards. The Judge rejected the standards as not having the force of law and we had to prove from point one that the timber was fit for purpose. The present situation his highly desirable.[5]

These H levels are now so well ingrained in the memory of specifiers that it would be hard to imagine that any designer used to working with timber would need to refer to AS1604.1 or the myriad of proprietary lists that are circulating. Despite this apparent simplicity, we have observed that designers are experiencing the same misunderstandings about the efficacy and practicality of treatments on a recurring basis. This Guide will try to steer the reader through some complex issues. Problems with specifying timber treatment and problems with durability often come about through inexperienced designers reading and trying to apply the Standard without understanding it. Industry hazard lists are simplified and generally have more user-friendly information than the Australian Standard.[6] Specifying according to the Standard brings with it an expectation that something meaningful, achievable and desirable is being specified.

The issue is more clouded over recent years with the introduction of Codemarked timber, a *Performance Solution*[7] which meets the Performance Requirements of the NCC. For Class 1 buildings (standalone domestic or residential), in all states, excluding Queensland, the definition of structural stability and resistance in my opinion lacks clarity with the NCC speaking of "appropriate degree of reliability" and its need to "perform adequately."[8] The Queensland variation of the NCC is very explicit and requires 50 years termite resistance in Queensland.[9] A very valuable document is produced by the Queensland Government, which is also a primary document under the Queensland variations to the NCC called *Construction Timbers in Queensland*[10] gives instructions on how to achieve this life span and refers to the Hazard Levels in AS1604.1 without mentioning the AS1604.1 by name. The climatic zones in CTIQ have application nationwide.

---

[5] This case involved legal argument over bicycle bells from the 1800's and eventual damages of $150.

[6] E.g. Arch Chemicals, *Ecowood – Good for Generations to Come* (U.D.) brochure has recommendations that are different from AS1604 for boardwalks over fresh and saltwater. Similar recommendations to Arch's can be found on manufacturers' websites such as that of Riverland Treated Pine http://www.riverlandtreatedpine.com.au/FAQ.html. (Accessed 11 December 2010 and Gunns Timber products http://www.gunnstimber.com.au/products/pine/treatedPineKilnDried/index.php (Accessed December 11, 2010).

[7] Section B10

[8] P2.1.1

[9] QLD P2.1.3.

[10] Available at https://www.publications.qld.gov.au/dataset/construction-timbers-in-queensland

2 HAZARD LEVELS AND TIMBER

Preservation Specifications

The treatment of timber with preservatives is concerned mainly with the protection of sapwood. The amount of preservative required in the timber is expressed as its Retention Level. With the repeal of Queensland's *Timber Utilisation and Marketing Act* (TUMA) and the New South Wales *Timber Marketing Act* (TMA) there is now only one legislated standard that specifies the required minimum retention levels for specific hazards and end uses. The national standard is AS1604.1 (2012), a companion document to the National Construction Code (NCC) formerly the Building Code of Australia (BCA). The terminology used to describe the six main exposure and biological hazards are:

Hazard Level: Exposure & Biological Hazard AS1604.1-2012	Typical Use
H1 – Interior above ground, completely protected from weather and well ventilated: Beetles and borers only	Framing, flooring, furniture, interior joinery
H2 – Interior above ground. Partially protected from wetting. Termites and borers only (Further comments are made below on H2)	Framing, flooring
H3 – Exterior above ground subject to periodic wetting. Decay, termites and borers	Weatherboards, fascia, window joinery, exterior framing and decking
H4 – Exterior in ground. Subject to severe wetting. Decay, termites and borers	Fencing, greenhouses, pergolas and landscaping timbers
H5 – Exterior in ground, with or in fresh water. Decay, termites and borers	Retaining walls, piling, house stumps, building poles, cooling tower fill
H6 – SW and NW marine water exposure. Marine borers	Boat hulls, marine piles, jetty cross bracing, landing steps.

Table 2. Hazard levels.

Where protection against borers is prime consideration, the Australian code has only one hazard level, H1 as listed above, but the matching New Zealand standard (NZ3640) has a sub-category of hazard level, H1.2 which is for protection where there is the addition of a moderate risk of dampness or water, i.e. a leak in the bathroom. It is rare to see our H1 (or H1.1 as it is known over the Tasman) treated timber there.[11]

Within any particular charge of timber in a treatment cylinder, a range of preservative penetrations and retentions will be achieved depending on the moisture content, sapwood to heartwood ratio, species, treatment schedule and inclusion of additives. This range should be understood as presenting acceptable and better treatment as opposed to unsatisfactory and satisfactory treatment. Table Two shows the hazard levels for different applications.

AS1604.1 provides strict guidelines for the minimum amount of chemical preservative required in the sapwood of timber, its penetration into the sapwood and often also the heartwood in order for the wood to perform as we expect. The longstanding penetration requirements which were based on In Ground Durability had to be changed in the 2010 edition to bring further clarity. With the release of *AS 5604-*

---

[11] Branz. *Timber Treatment.* URL: https://www.weathertight.org.nz/new-buildings/timber-treatment/ Date Accessed: September 20, 2020.

2005 Timber - Natural durability ratings there was a time when an In Ground Durability 3, in many cases now also classed as an Above Ground 2, could, through a cursory read of the 2000 edition of standard, have been treated inappropriately. The updated penetration requirements for the different Hazard Levels for mainly waterborne preservatives are tabled below.

Hazard	Durability	Sapwood	Heartwood
H1	1 to 4	100%	Penetration not required
H2	1 to 4	100%	Penetration not required if termite resistant otherwise 5 mm (<35mm) 8 mm (>35) envelope
H3	1 AGD	100%	Penetration not required
	2 to 4 AGD		5 mm (<35mm) 8 mm (>35) envelope
H4	1 and 2 IGD	100%	Penetration not required
	3 and 4 IGD		10 mm envelope
H5	1 and 2 IGD	100%	Penetration not required
	3 and 4 IGD		20 mm envelope
H6	Turpentine		Penetration not required
	All others		20 mm envelope[12]
Table 3.	Penetration of heartwood with preservatives (excludes H2F).		

Excluded from Table 3 is H2F, a special designation for pine framing treatment introduced in 2010 for areas where the *Mastotermes darwiniensis*, or giant northern termite, is not active. As part of this change, slash pine, which has heartwood with natural termite resistance, was exempted from the heartwood penetration requirements that were applied to say radiata. Unlike the penetration requirements listed in Table 3, the penetration requirements for H2F vary depending to the preservative used: This timber is often identified by the addition of a blue colouring.

Chemical	Penetration of sapwood	Penetration of non-termite resistant heartwood on outside of piece	Penetration of Termite resistant heartwood on outside of piece
Permethrin	5 mm	5 mm	Not required
Bifenthrin	2 mm	2 mm	Not required
Imidacloprid	2 mm	2 mm	Not required
Table 4.	Penetration requirements for H2F[13]		

While this all seems straightforward, and indeed should be, specifiers, resellers, builders and certifiers need to be extremely cautious and still read manufacturer's guidelines. The definition of H3 treatment from AS1604,1 is "outside, above ground, subject to periodic moderate wetting and leaching." Suitable applications given in the standard are fascia, pergolas, windows, framing and decking.[14] Yet one supplier of H3 LVL says on their literature "LOSP H3 Not recommended for use in external, exposed applications unless installed with effective moisture protection." Compare that with the standard's

---

[12] The H6 requirements are very simplified.
[13] AS 1604.1-2012, 3.2.2 and Table H2.1
[14] AS1604.1-2012, Table 1.1.

definition of H2, "Inside, above ground protected from wetting and no leaching."[15] These applications are framing used in dry situations. Well, I suppose I studied too much philosophy where importance is given to the meaning of words but quite frankly, I cannot see too much difference between that suppliers permitted "H3" use and the formal definition of H2. Further, that supplier excludes some applications that are specifically mentioned in the H3 application of AS1604.1. H3 is supposed to be H3 so let the buyer beware.

---

[15] AS1604.1-2012, Table 1.1

3 COMMON TREATMENT OPTIONS

Waterborne VPI Preservatives

Understand Figure 3 and you understand the strength and limitations all commercially available waterborne timber treatments in Australia.[17] This figure shows the end of an untreated powerpole which has been sprayed with a dye to differentiate the sapwood from the heartwood (sometimes called truewood).

Figure 4 and Figure 5 respectively show a microscopic view of the sapwood and heartwood of tallowwood. It is evident that the vessels in the sapwood are porous allowing the treatment chemicals to flow through them. By contrast, the vessels in the heartwood are blocked. These occlusions are called tyloses. To effectively treat the powerpole shown in

Figure 3.   Sapwood/heartwood, the key to understanding waterborne timber treatment.[16]

Figure 3, in my South East Queensland climate I needed to dry it for at least 4-6 weeks to remove some free moisture from the sapwood, place it in an autoclave, draw a high vacuum and the porous sapwood empties of air and then flood the autoclave with treatment solution. The vacuum inside the wood very quickly draws the preservative into the sapwood. Finally, I topped off with some pressure. This is called the "full cell" process.

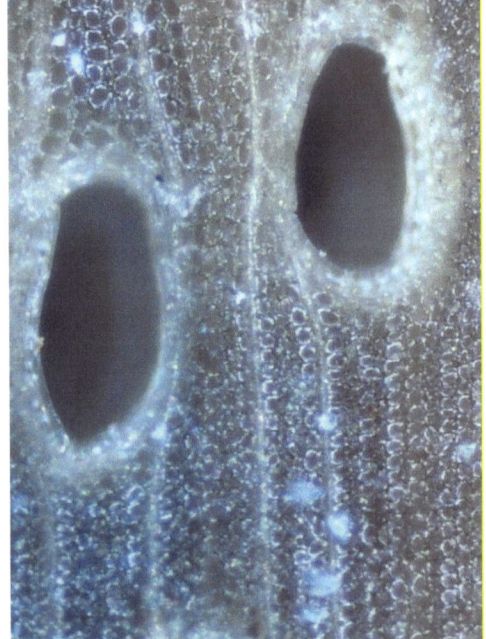

Figure 4.   Empty sapwood vessels

Figure 5.   Plugged heartwood vessels

---

[16] Note the bands of truewood in the sapwood which can make chemical analysis of samples awkward as there is no treatment in these areas. These untreatable areas are counted in the sample that is analysed.

[17] E.g. CCA, ACQ, Tanalith E and, boron.

Even with the further application of as much vacuum and pressure as you can achieve, and pumping for protracted periods, the solution will still not pass from the sapwood into the heartwood.[18] While there are different processes using more recent solvent-borne technology, the large majority of treatment in Australia is with waterborne treatments. While the process of treating with waterborne preservatives is old technology, it remains good and cheap technology. However, it does have some limitations. These are:

- Some species simply cannot be treated reliably with this process and they should not be offered to the public as "treated" timber. They are known as refractory species and were listed under the regulations of TUMA.[19] Examples of refractory species are white cypress and Douglas fir
- The sapwood swells during the treatment process and has to be redried. This is particularly an issue with pine
- The green or brown colour "advertises" the presence of preservative and
- The cost of treating pine, particularly with some of the CCA replacements, is high.

These drawbacks have led to the increasing popularity of different ways of treatment, the most common in domestic settings being light organic solvent preservation (LOSP).

Waterborne Dipping and Spraying
The introduction of H2F hazard level in AS1604.1-2010 for applications south of the Tropic of Capricorn set the stage for a revolution in timber preservation. There was now an alternative to previous high level of penetration which varied from 5 to 8 mm depending on thickness and which involved considerable expense to produce. At the time of writing, there were roughly two million m^3 of pine framing timber used per annum in Australia and of that, roughly 60% (900,000 m^3 locally produced and the balance imported) is treated with surface applied preservatives to H2F or an equivalent through Codemarked processes. (The treatment of imported timber is important for control of the European house borer). Protection is normally achieved through a waterborne preservative which is applied through spraying, dipping and sometimes in an autoclave (where LOSP would be used). In a sawmill setting the preservative is likely to be applied by spraying as part of the inline process and an importer is likely to dip the whole pack.

Unlike the VPI process, because the amount of water involved with spraying is small, and period of time that the timber is in contact with the timber in dipping is small and there is no vacuum and pressure assistance, there is minimal dimension change. Treating pine in a VPI plant can involve double strapping. A tight set are needed for transit and packing the plant, but they need to be cut prior to treatment when the timber expends. Failing to do this would see damage to the timber and likely the straps will break. With dipping, the straps just tighten a little. Pine treated using the VPI process also often needs to be re-dried.

Preservatives applied by dipping or spraying only require a shallow penetration to achieve an effective

---

[18] Penetration is said to be possible, but the pressure required is 1000 lb per sq inch, Wallis, Norman K. *Australian Timber Handbook*. (Sydney: Angus and Robinson, 1956), 221.
[19] Keith R Bootle's *Wood in Australia, Second Edition* (North Ryde: McGraw Hill Australia, 2005) gives the suitability of a species for treatment under its species notes. Note that this recommendation is accurate in regard to waterborne preservatives but not necessarily for solventborne e.g. White Cypress p. 270. Incising can allow preservation of refractory species and is common overseas.

envelope penetration. Bifenthrin and imidacloprid only needs a 2 mm envelope while permethrin requires 5 mm (refer Table 4 for full penetration requirements). This is a very economical process due to the low uptake of chemical and the ability to be used in process and this is all done without any loss of efficacy! The preservatives are highly effective and additional protection is achieved when using permethrin and bifenthrin as they are also repellants.[20]

Light Organic Solvent Preservatives

A light organic solvent preservative (LOSP) derives its name from the solvent, originally white spirit, which is used to carry a range of organic insecticides and fungicides. The treatment is generally, though not always, clear but often has colours added to distinguish the hazard level. Solventborne preservatives are mainly used to preserve softwoods used in H1 through to H3 applications. This process differs to the more common VPI process as, instead of using vacuum and the pressure, LOSP uses a double vacuum where the initial vacuum draws the chemical into the timber and a second vacuum draws off the excess. Unlike the VPI process also, which keeps adding the treatment solution till the timber will accept no more, the double vacuum process usually stops after a target uptake of solution has been reached. Unlike treatment of hardwoods which has traditionally been done on unseasoned timber, LOSP is only used with seasoned product. Because the solvent does not wet the timber, which would otherwise cause it to swell, it means that timber can be treated after all processing has been completed.

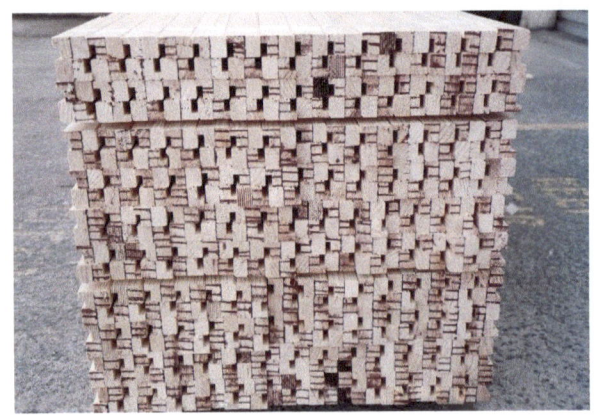

Figure 6.   Fully prefinished joinery components ready to be LOSP treated

It was for exactly this stability that the first plants were imported from the UK. Australian timber window manufacturers had seen such plants in the UK and understood that this process allowed them to treat fully prefinished components for window frames etc., just prior to assembly (Figure 6). Protim, the original supplier, bought in the first plants in 1977 and used a formula called "Protim 80 WR" which was a mixture of pentachlorophenol (PCP), tributyltin oxide (TBTO) as the fungicide and dieldrin as the insecticide. Those active ingredients have now been replaced by less toxic and more environmentally friendly organic actives.[21] These replacement chemicals include synthetic pyrethroids and imidacloprid as the insecticides and azoles or copper naphthenates as the fungicides. The white spirit has also largely been replaced with high flash kerosene.

Protim initially claimed a 20 mm penetration of the end grain and, as the lateral surfaces dried quickly and posed a low risk of decay, they were able to give a 25-year guarantee for products manufactured with their LOSP treatment providing it was further supplemented by a good quality paint or stain. That guarantee was remarkable as these windows, and the like, were being made from no more than meranti! A positive aspect of this treatment was that there was no contaminated sawdust or shavings to dispose of. Despite the widespread use of timber windows being a thing of the past the process has remained as different applications were found.[22] Painting was part of original requirements for the Protim guarantee

---

[20] Norton, Jack. *Pers. Com.* 26 September 2020.
[21] Greenacre, Edward. *Pers. Com.* 9 and 11 September, 2020. Edward established the Protim LOSP business in Australia.
[22] Greenacre, Edward. Pers. Com. 9 and 11 September, 2020.

and was driven in part also by uncertainty about whether UV would break down TBTO,[23] Irrespective of the preservative, for all H3 applications, LOSP should still be used in conjunction with "an appropriate finish system to inhibit mould growth on the surface and reduce the effects of weathering".[24] Very importantly, this finishing system must be maintained. Weathering can be reduced on a short-term basis through the addition of waxes and resins, but these can cause problems with subsequent coating systems. Residual solvents may also interfere with paint systems.

Figure 7. Decay in LOSP treated handrails.

Some LOSP applications have not been as universally successful as hoped such as primed pine handrail but this is generally, if not always due to inappropriate construction practices rather than the effectiveness of the treatment. These handrails are sold in 5.4 metre lengths and cut to the required length on site and in doing so lose the end penetration which was one of the original reasons for introducing LOSP. (With an LVL joist there is a 150 mm end grain requirement for envelope treatment)[25] Effectively, after onsite cutting there is now no penetration of LOSP into the end grain so good building and sales practice becomes paramount. Figure 7 shows a handrail with severe decay after 15 years. It was evident one year earlier and, having felt all the "spongy" ends in the 20 plus panels, it was evident that the decay was present under the paint a long time before it was visible. My experience has been that builders tended to treat the treated LOSP treated pine handrail as they did a rail made from the heartwood of durable hardwoods, i.e., they simply sealed the cut ends with paint. Poor sales practice through not selling the appropriate sealers contributed, no doubt driven by the same lack of product knowledge.[26]

---

[23] Norton, Jack. *Pers. Com.* 2 October 2020.

[24] Timber Queensland. *Technical Data Sheet 22, Light Organic Solvent Preservative Treated Timber* (March 2014), 1. I would consider an "approved paint system" to be one that has been approved under the Australian Paint Approval Scheme (APAS). The APAS is administered by the Commonwealth Scientific & Industrial Research Organisation (CSIRO) and is believed to be of a higher standard than the Australian Standard. Approved paints will carry the APAS approval on its label.

[25] AS1604.4 Clause 7.4

[26] When we operated a hardware store, we sold many pieces of LOSP treated handrail. Sadly, not one of our suppliers advised that we needed the preservative and not one of our customers asked for it either. I may have sold the piece in the image.

Figure 8. Clear and coloured aerosol type end sealers necessary for LOSP treated timber

For H3 applications, it is necessary to seal with an "approved" or "appropriate"[27] preservative, not paint. Timber Queensland recommends brush on preservatives[28] which, strictly, would include CN oil and emulsion and while these products will work well, they are likely to have compatibility issues with topcoats. Two other products manufactured by Lonza (Figure 8) that are approved with their LOSP treatments but do not have compatibility issues are *Ecoseal,* a copper and permethrin spray with a greenish colour or *Endseal,* another spray which uses zinc naphthenate and permethrin. *Endseal* has the advantage of showing where the timber has been sealed. Other preservative end sealers such as Koppers Performance Chemical's *Protim Timbercare XJ* are also available. It is doubtful that these spray on sealers will be as effective as the 150 mm penetration required under AS1604.4 for veneer-based product and which is generally achieved in a factory setting but should still provide sufficient protection.

It is common for LOSP treated pine products such as handrails and doorjambs to be pre-primed with water-based primer, but this primer is not always of high quality. A poor-quality primer will affect the performance of the finishing system needed to protect the timber. In the absence of product branding and/or painting finish guidelines, the paint quality can be checked by scribing an "X" on the painted surface, firmly applying adhesive tape over it and then lifting. If any paint adheres to the tape, then all the primer should be removed and repainted with oil-based primer.[29] Without a preservative being applied to the end, painting can compound the decay problem, not avert it. Fine cracks in the paint let in moisture and slow down its escape. Research by DPI Forestry in Queensland has shown that painted and unmaintained housed joints in the weather, decay more rapidly than unpainted.[30]

---

[27] Manufacturer's recommendations can use vague terminology. The purchaser should ask for a specific product.

[28] Timber. *Technical 22* …, 1.

[29] Timber. *Technical 22*..., 1- 2. This is also in keeping with the Australian Paint Manufacturers Federation Fact Sheet T4 "Preparation of LOSP Pre-Primed Timber" dated February 1 2007 and also found summarised in Solver Paints *Product information sheet LOSP Treated Pre Primed Timber SS-127*.

[30] Francis, Lesley P and Jack Norton. *Above-Ground Durability Estimation in Australia, Results after 16 Years Exposure*, Document IRG/WP 05-20314. Paper given at the 36th Annual Conference of the International Research Group on Wood Protection, Bangalore April 2005, 10ff.

Notwithstanding poor building and sales practice there was an issue, at times, with the effectiveness of the treatment itself. The failure of an LOSP treated pine rafter in a shelter shed is shown in Figure 9. It was treated to H3 under the requirements of the 1997 edition of AS1604.1 and even the later 2000 edition did not mention any requirement for painting the timber. While painting was seen as desirable, and probably necessary, the difficulty in specifying, enforcing and interpreting a requirement for painting meant that it was only incorporated in the 2010 standard but was part of TUMA.[31]

Figure 9.   Failure of LOSP treated timber after 12 years but practice and codes have changes since then.

One of the most common treatment then was tributyltin either as an oxide (TBTO) or naphthenate (TBTN). The 2010 version of the standard required double the amount TBTO or TBTN if the timber was unpainted.[32] Commenting on this change, the later Standard notes, "These values represent the Committee's judgment based on the assessment of the best information available at the time."[33] This is not a strong vote of confidence![34] This is the only preservative in the standard which has a different amount of chemical for unpainted and painted product. This product has not been used for a few years in Australia and is proposed to be removed from the next edition of AS1604.1.

There is some use of LOSP in hardwood specified in AS1604.1, e.g., for H1 borer protection in Victorian Ash. My own experience was less than satisfactory. We had been exporting 88x19 spotted gum decking to Japan but the colour of the treatment in the sapwood, first CCA then Tanalith E[35] was causing buyer resistance. We saw LOSP as an answer as it was clear and would give the impression that the timber was not treated. We kiln dried some sappy 100x25 spotted gum to 10-12% moisture content, dressed it to profile and sent it to an LOSP plant in Brisbane for treating. When we sent samples to the laboratory for testing, we found they failed penetration requirements! On a practical basis we could do no more than this so let the idea, which sounded excellent in theory, slide. Later, Arch assured us that this would have been caused by an inappropriate schedule[36] at the treatment plant, not with the practicality of

---

[31] Cookson L, M Hedley. *Adequacy of H3 LOSP tin based preservative treatment for exposed external structural uses*. (Melbourne: Australian Government, 2005) 18.

[32] Compare AS1604.1-2000, Table H3 with AS1604.1-2010 Table h3, note clause 4.4.

[33] AS1604.1-2010 Clause 4.4.

[34] This is not too harsh a judgement as "there is still some uncertainty as to the performance of 0.16% m/m tin (it has not been tested) although it should be a significant improvement over 0.08% m/m tin." Cookson. *Adequacy ...*, 3.

[35] Alternatively known as Copper Azole in Australia and in the US as Wolman E or Copper Boron Azole (CBA).

[36] This is the term used in the trade to describe the solution strengths, times (or trigger points), pressure and vacuum used to produce a batch of treated timber. It was probably mixed with a charge of pine which uses a different schedule.

achieving the required result. One producer, N.K. Collins of Toowoomba,[37] who wanted to achieve the same, non-treated look, had reported success with 19 mm white cypress domestic decking, a species that is notoriously difficult, if not impossible to treat with waterborne preservatives.[38]

Figure 10. Decay in Victorian ash laminated beam ends.

The normal use of LOSP treatment for H2 applications would require it to be used in conjunction with a species that has natural termite resistance and H3 hardwood would be restricted to Durability One Above Ground species to AS5604 such as spotted gum and ironbark. Lower termite resistant or durability timbers must have the heartwood penetrated by at least 5 to 8 mm (depending on the thickness), normally an impossibility, or the untreated section be not more than 20% of the cross-section area.[39] From experience, it is likely to be closer to 80% on larger structural sizes. One chemical supplier adds penetration enhancers to the preservative which allows Victorian ash to be sold as H3. I have no personal experience with this product and will only comment on actual samples provided. With Victorian ash, any post treatment working and cutting to length may expose Durability 3 Above Ground timber which is likely to decay (Figure 10). Construction with this H3 timber requires careful attention to detail such as end capping.[40] Notably, I understand that, at the time of writing, not all chemical suppliers have been able to develop an LOSP product that consistently conforms to the H3 hardwood penetration requirements of AS1604.1.

Glueline Preservatives

A mindset change among LVL and plywood manufacturers led to the demand for a new preservative process. The two main factors that were forefront in their thinking was economics and ownership. If biocides could be added to the glueline without modifying existing manufacturing lines, there would be efficiency gains through having fewer steps in the manufacturing process. This brought with it a reduction in the costs and delays associated with second party treatment. By not having to rely on a second party for a crucial manufacturing stage, post treatment, better in-house control could be achieved, and the producer would then and have control of all stages of manufacture so giving total ownership of what they produced. The producer would have the potential to control the retention of the preservatives more tightly as they could be accurately weighed when being added to the glue.[41]

Apart from the additional costs and loss of control, post gluing treatment in conventional plants could have their own issues such as the need for residual solvents to dry or, should a waterbased formulation be used, the need to re-dry. The intention with glueline preservation was that sufficient preservative

---

[37] Unfortunately, no longer trading.
[38] Jack Norton commented that he had not seen an example of a successful LOSP penetration of Cypress and that waterborne treatment was an impossibility. Extreme caution must be exercised with this species.
[39] AS 1604.1-2012, 4.2.
[40] Vicbeam. *Vic ash H3 Hardwood.* URL: https://vicbeam.com.au/product-services/gl18-vic-ash-h3-hardwood/ Date accessed: September 16, 2020.
[41] Norton, Jack. *Pers. Com.* 26 September 2020.

would diffuse the full depth into each veneer and that the pressure that is applied during the pressing process could assist this migration.[42] This would be further assisted by micro cracking that arose during the peeling process.

About 20 years prior to writing, glueline preservatives did become available on the Australian market but the addition of preservative to glue did not prove to be a straightforward matter of adding already approved formulations as some interfered with the development of the glue bond. As well, the adhesives themselves could prove to be aggressive because of their very high pH which, coupled with the extreme heat and pressure of the pressing process, could breakdown organic preservatives such as bifenthrin before they diffused in the timber. These initial difficulties have been largely overcome and there has been rapid progress in this area of preservation. Approvals are in place for applications ranging from H1 to H3. Permethrin and bifenthrin, common active ingredients in the preservatives, as has been mentioned, have always been repellants[43] but some are now promoting this, quite reasonably, as a dual defense against insect attack.[44] It is now also possible to purchase glueline preservatives where the active ingredients are in microcapsules with a polymer wall that protects it from the extremes of pH, heat and pressure.[45] At the same time these polymers still allow the preservative to be released and bond to the wood fibre.[46] An additional benefit of encapsulation minimizes the risk of contact with the chemical during manufacture and construction.

LOSP treatment, as has been mentioned, is effective, but it requires close compliance to the manufacturer's instructions for sealing end grain and on site cutting. Timber that has been treated with glueline preservatives that reach the core can, potentially, be drilled and cut on site without the need for re-treatment. With the preservatives diffusing from the glue line it only must reach halfway through the laminate to successfully reach the core except for the external laminate. As a first line of defence, the manufacturers recommendation for treatment of the exterior laminates of the beam must be followed closely and this may involve the addition of a paint on anti-fungal biocides[47] or be painted if they are exposed to the weather. Also, the manufacturers guidelines for resealing cut ends should be followed.[48] It should not be assumed that all manufactures guidelines are the same and that there can be a simple product substitution based on price without checking any change of instructions.[49]

Tar Oil Preservatives

Creosote is the earliest preservative used in the commercial preservation industry. The preservative value of less refined products from coal was known as early as 1681 and a patent for preserving timber with creosote using the full cell method was granted in 1838 to John Bethell. This is the treatment process described earlier under waterborne treatments and is sometimes called by his name. Creosote, derived

---

[42] Lonza. *Azotek, Glueline based protection for LVL and I-Beams against insects and decay*. (Otahuhu: Lonza, 2017) 1.

[43] Norton, Jack. *Pers. Com.* 26 September 2020.

[44] Koppers Determite H2S is an example

[45] Lonza's Permatek^{tm} 100 encaps is an example.

[46] Lonza. *Permatek, Solutions for the control of insects in engineered Wood Products*. (Otahuhu: Lonza, 2017) 2.

[47] Lonza. *Azotek …*, 1.

[48] Lonza's Azotek, a New Zealand H2.1 treatment does not need end sealing but Koppers deterMite, while again not insisting on end sealing states that it is "good building practice to do so." Koppers. deterMite H2S, Reasons to choose deterMite. URL: https://www.kopperspc.com.au/determite-h2s/top-reasons.html Date accessed: September 25, 2020.

[49] A review of different supplier's guidelines found differences in the areas where they could be used as well as painting and end sealing guidelines.

from the high temperature distillation of coal tar, is a very complex compound with over 100 constituent chemicals.[58] While individually none of its constituents is particularly effective, there appears to be a synergism between the aromatic hydrocarbons and phenolic compounds. These compounds effectively protect timber against decay, insect and marine organism attack.[59] It is reasonable to call it a "dirty" process because of its strong odour, its propensity to soil clothes and produce burns similar to sunburn on skin exposed to contact. This is further compounded by the tendency for creosote treated timber to bleed for some time after treatment. These bleeds can form tar-like deposits known in the trade as "crud" which, because of their fungitoxic effect, should not be removed.[60]

In Australia, creosote is listed by the APVMA under Schedule 7 of the Standard for the Uniform Scheduling of Drugs and Poisons (SUSDP), based on concerns about carcinogenicity.[61] The primary concern, benzo-α-pryene (BaP), is fairly common in the environment and has been reported at up to 1000 times the concentration in car exhausts than in the air at a creosote treatment plant.[62] Australian high temperature creosote contains much less than 50 ppm of BaP.[63]

Creosote's long track record has proved it to be a highly effective preservative[64] but, despite the effectiveness, its overall popularity as a preservative has understandably diminished. At the time of writing there are only two plants in Australia using high temperature creosote.[65] Some of the traditional uses for creosote were for poles and railway sleepers but creosote is seldom used for this now in Australia. While creosote has no place in domestic timber applications, it is still meeting a strong demand in the agricultural sector.

---

[58] Campbell-McFarlane, Jacqueline. *Creosote and its Use as a Wood Preservative*. U.S. Environment Protection Agency http://www.epa.gov/pesticides/factsheets/chemicals/creosote_main.htm. Accessed April 10, 2012. The actual composition of creosote varies greatly around the world.

[59] Mai, C. and Militz, H. Chemical Wood Protection in *Wood Production, Wood Technology, and Biotechnological Impacts*. Kues, Ursula (Ed). (Universitatsverlag Gottingen, 2007), 261.

[60] Greaves, H. Pigment Emulsified Creosote (PEC) – Improved Oil-Based Preservatives. *Ann. Rev. Div. Chem. & Wood Technol* (CSIRO,1985), 26.

[61] APVMA. Creosote. http://www.apvma.gov.au/products/review/completed/creosote.php. Accessed April 11, 2012.

[62] Greaves, Harry. *Current Trends in protection of Timber*. 13th All Australia Timber Congress Nov 1990, 7.

[63] Greaves. *Current...*, 7. He reported that, at the time he wrote the EEC classed BaP content from 50-1000 ppm as harmful but not toxic.

[64] An industry source commented, "I think creosote products have performed better [than CCA] over the years, mainly because they were over treated in the first instance". *Pers. Com.* April 11, 2012.

[65] High temperature (distilled at the high temperature of 900-1300 C) creosote is solid below approx. 40 C and is usually maintained at 90-100 C for treating. The VPI process is used. This is opposed to the "high temperature" hot and cold bath (open tank) process. An unregistered creosote plant using this process was established a few kilometres from the writer's home. The creosote caught fire one night!

Figure 11. Creosote treated horse fences.

Creosote treated timber has some distinct advantages over CCA. Pine treated with CCA can be more brittle than if it was treated with creosote. Livestock do not like the taste of creosote and so do not chew it, a problem with CCA. The oil also works as a water repellent. Further, while CCA treated timber continues to burn after the ignition source has been removed, aged creosote treated timber is less likely to catch alight.[66] One manufacturer, Koppers, claims that it performs even better than CCA in acid sulphate soils.[67] It might be described as a H5+ treatment especially as it controls some forms of rot, (e.g. soft rot), for which CCA gives inadequate protection.[68] Practical disadvantages are poor paintability and glueability with normal products. Despite these difficulties, gluing processes have been developed in the US for repairing railway bridges.[69]

Given the popularity of creosote in southern states it is curious that it was/is rare in Queensland. This is partly explained through Queensland unions placing an embargo on creosote for many applications such as powerpoles but that does not explain why it is not used widely in rural applications.

A modification of creosote treatment is Pigment Emulsified Creosote (PEC). This process was developed in Australia by the CSIRO in collaboration with Koppers. The input of Electrical Trades Union, which had an obvious interest in a safer treatment, surely was unique. PEC is comprised of roughly 70% high temperature tar oils in water emulsion along with high quality controlled micronised (reducing the particle size) colouring agents.[70] The colouring agents are not used primarily as a colourant, instead they help lock in the active constituents of the preservative which are inclined to bleed, especially in hot weather. PEC is claimed to be easier to handle than straight creosote. The oil is still heated but to about 30 degrees C less, giving substantial energy savings and partly offsetting the higher material cost. The surface of PEC treated timber is less sticky and the oils do not easily exude from the

---

[66] Wilkinson, J.G. *Industrial Timber Preservation*. (London: Associated Business Press, 1979), 133. If a fire is established it burns more vigorously and with more smoke than untreated wood. This precludes its use in mining.

[67] Koppers Wood Products Pty. Ltd. *Treated Hardwood Foundation Piles - Case Studies. Rev 0, 2009.* 3, 6.

[68] In Australia, one variety of brown rot is resistant to creosote. Most decay in Europe is due to one form of Brown Rot and in the US most degradation is from a number of forms of brown rot. Bagley, S.T. and D.L. Richter. Biodegredation of Brown Rot Fungi in *The Mycota, A Comprehensive Treatise on Fungi as Experimental Systems for Basic and Applied Research Vol 10 Industrial Applications*. Ed. By Karl Esser, Joan W. Bennett, H. D. Osiewacz. (Berlin: Springer-Verlaq, 2002), 338. Australian Brown rot is related.

[69] Tingley, Dan. *Pers. Com.* April 14, 2012.

[70] Greaves. *Pigment...*, 27. Mai describes the European version of PEC as using 80% medium temperature creosote which only has a low smell intensity. *Chemical...*, 262-3. Medium creosote is also reported as having a lower incidence of the potential carcinogen BaP, Greaves. *Environmental...*, 7.

timber.[71] Acceptable surfaces have been achieved within days of treating.[72] On top of all this, the odour is far less than with normal creosote. PEC treatment is used in conjunction with CCA to produce double treated marine plies for temperate and tropical waters. PEC is a much cleaner version of creosote but like HTC, it also causes problems when it comes in contact with the skin.

The many advantages of PEC over straight creosote ensure that PEC will continue to have an important place in the Australian market despite its cost. When combined with CCA, PEC remains the only option for marine piles in warmer waters.

Envelope Protection of Natural Rounds

With the untreated pole end in Figure 3, it doesn't matter that heartwood cannot be penetrated with the preservative as there is a complete circle or "envelope" of preservative encasing the heartwood. If there are no cuts or holes put through the treated sapwood the pole is "preserved". Durability through preservation is only achievable on a practical basis in natural rounds with at least an unbroken 12mm sapwood envelope.[73]

While there may be no real difference between a house stump and a powerpole in that they are both H5 applications the treatment requirements are not the same. Poles are produced under AS2209 and require what might be called a H5+ treatment. There is a far more rigid species identification requirement to confirm the Durability Class and width of the sapwood band.[74] The treatment levels may vary also depending on customer requirements and may be higher than a normal H5 treatment. Further, there is a tight quality and straightness specification. For structural H5 hardwood applications, specifiers are better referring to AS2209 than AS1604. This happens automatically if rounds are purchased from manufacturers who also manufacture poles.

---

[71] Mai. *Chemical...*, 262-3.
[72] Greaves. *Pigment...*, 32. Though a small minority of product inexplicitly still continued to exude creosote.
[73] AS3818.11-2009 5.2. (a). Blackbutt only has a narrow sapwood band so the 12mm restriction can be an issue with that species. Ironbark by comparison also has a narrow sapwood band but has natural durability so it would be misleading to think of a pole in that species has been "preserved" through treatment. Durability 4 in ground poles requires a 35mm sapwood barrier but no penetration into the heartwood. Compare that to no minimum and 20mm respectively with AS1604.1, see Table 3 above.
[74] Some Durability 2 in ground species may not have the minimum 12mm sapwood band. The width of the band is not an issue if you do actually have a Durability 1 in ground timber.

4 EFFECTIVENESS OF TREATMENT

Treatment's Effectiveness on Natural Hardwood Rounds.

Termite Attack   External Decay   Internal Decay

Figure 12.   Groundline degrade. Images represent extreme examples. Poles would not normally get to this condition.

Generally speaking, natural hardwood rounds with sapwood treated to H5 can expect a life span of 25 to 50 years.[75] This life expectancy is defined more closely[76] in AS/NZS7000 as 45 to 55 years for In-Ground Durability Class 1 poles and 35 to 45 years for Durability Class 2 poles. (Most poles are spotted gum which is In-Ground Durability 2.).[77] When determining the whole of life cost of major public infrastructure such as our power distribution network, there is a vast economic difference between the high and low end of the generally accepted span or even the ten year span of AS/NZS7000 between Durability 1 and 2 poles. The design life of a power pole in South East Queensland in the ENERGEX area is 50 years[78], the top of this range. The service life is another matter. Because lines are constantly being upgraded and therefore the poles being removed from service for reasons other than failure, it is difficult to state an accurate service life. However, it is believed to be in excess of 40 years.[79]

---

[75] It was found initially that CCA treated poles "were less effective in service than previously expected". Leightley, *Technical...*, 10.

[76] Table D4.

[77] Robson, Peter. *Pers. Com.* August 15, 2011. Mr. Robson was Senior Engineer Maintenance Standards, Network Maintenance of ENERGEX at the time of the advice.

[78] Robson, Peter. *Pers. Com.* August 5, 2011. There may be a move in time to a 45 year life in accordance with AS/NZS7000.

[79] Robson. *Pers. Com...*, 2011.

It is only possible for ENERGEX to plan to achieve the upper end of the time range by a planned five yearly inspections and treatment, if necessary, at the groundline. This inspection looks for rot and termite activity. If degrade is found, Boron and Fluoride salts are applied. Pole bandages are an important part of the maintenance.[80] When poles reach 100% of the design strength (when the diameter reduces to about 80% but the calculation is complex) they are either removed or staked with steel "pole nails".[81] Given the effectiveness of pole bandages it is surprising they are not fitted at installation rather than after decay is present!

Figure 13.   Installing a pole bandage.

Figure 14.   Soft rot at groundline.

While CCA treatments are very effective, they are not totally effective against soft rot in all eucalypts[82] so inspections are critical. Any structures using H5 treated natural rounds cannot simply be installed and then forgotten. Like power poles, they must be subject to regular inspection and, if necessary, maintained. Figure 14 shows the effect of soft rot at ground-line.[83] When soft rot became an issue in Queensland, the retention requirements were substantially increased from 24 kg per m^3 to 30 kg per m^3.[84] It is likely that a modern CCA pole would have a better service life than one treated under TUPA (the predecessor to TUMA).

---

[80] Robson. *Pers. Com.* …., 2011.

[81] Robson. *Pers. Com.* …, 2011.

[82] Norton. *Pers. Com.* Sept 1, 2011. It was reported that high levels of CCA did not protect against soft rot attack but that the severity was lessened. Leightley. *Technical…,* 12. Some brown rots are an issue also.

[83] This image also appears in a paper presented at the *ESAA Pole Symposium,* Gold Coast, 1980 by H. Greaves and K.J. McCarthy entitled Inspection and Maintenance Procedures for Ground-Line Defects in Wood Poles. It is said to be of a eucalypt pole after 5 years' service!

[84] The requirements under the Timber Users Protection Act (TUPA) was 24kg per m^3 (Leightley, *Technical…,* 6) but was increased under its successor TUMA. The 30kg figure represents 1.2 (percent mass/mass for CCA treated hardwood x 2.7742 for Type C formulation for CCA /100 X 900kg density per m3 which equals 30kg m. Denser timber would have a higher requirement.

Treatment's Effectiveness on Sawn Hardwood

Figure 15 shows a pack of bollards prior to treatment. If you look carefully you will see that I have blocked in the sapwood with red. This is the only part of that pack that will be treated. It might be 5% of the total volume of that particular pack. It doesn't matter if you treat the sapwood to H3, H4, H5 or even H6. It has no effect on the remaining 95% of the timber. If the highlighted timber was simply missing, as in forklift damage, or allowed to decay, it would still meet all grades recognised under AS2082 Timber, Hardwood, visually stress graded.

Figure 15. Only the sections in red are treated.

To understand how little treatment can mean on sawn timber, consider the following: as a treater and processor, I can take a piece of blackbutt (Durability 2 in ground and, in our opinion and experience at the lower end of the group) without any sapwood, paint on some treatment chemical with a brush to colour it and I can still call it H5. I can then take it to a planer and dress off the external colouring and I can still call it H5! It is not the equal of a piece of spotted gum or ironbark with minimal sapwood treated to H3 even though AS5604.1 says it is.

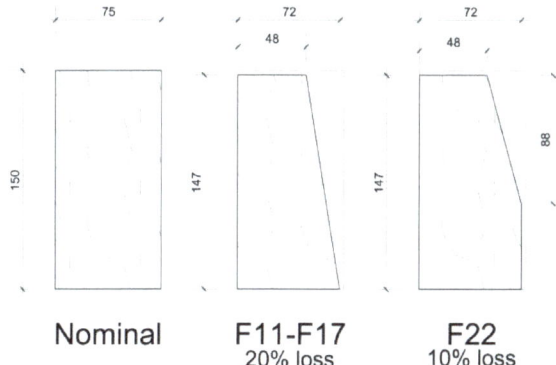

Figure 16. Permitted want and wane.[85]

Figure 16 shows what specifiers generally think they are specifying when they nominate 150x75 hardwood and what they are actually asking for. By far the majority of 75mm thick members[86] have so little sapwood on them that, with decay, it would meet the structural requirements of AS2082-2007. A specification that says "F14 hardwood treated to H5" then becomes virtually meaningless as a specification for structural timber. The key is to define the species correctly so the untreated 95% in this case (rarely is sapwood of structural members more than 15%) of the timber has suitable natural durability. Best practice in design and construction is still also essential.

The difference between the two types of treatment (envelope on rounds and partial treatment of sawn) is that blackbutt with an envelope protection has proven to be an acceptable powerpole whereas treated sawn blackbutt was never a good decking for a variety of reasons.[87]

---

[85] AS2082-2007, clauses 2.1.2 (n), 2.2.2 (n), 2.3.2 (n) and, 2.4.2 (n).
[86] The recommendation from OSA's Boardwalk Design Guide and Deckwood Selection Guide for any joists where a 14# screw is used is for a minimum 75mm width joist to avoid damage by the fasteners.
[87] As indicated by this species' exclusion from the older Queensland specifications for crossarms, Main Roads bridges and for railway sleepers.

Areas of Over-treatment in AS 1604.1

The revision of the preservative treatment standard in 2010 and 2012 still saw the issue of overtreatment of sawn members found in the previous standard continue with classifications that are not achievable. An example of the impossibility is the requirement of H6 for boat building. The penetration requirements cannot be achieved in either hardwood or pine. This is an area where users can only rely on natural durability or on alternative methods such as anti-fouling paint. Notation to this effect should have been made in any revised standard.

Over-treatment is found in the requirement for decking. Bridge decking is required to be treated to H5, wharf decking to H5, jetty decking to H4 (down from H5 in the 2000 standard) and H3 for patios.[88] The last comes with a note that CCA treatment is not acceptable for this application due to [Australian Pesticides and Veterinary Medicines Authority (APVMA)] requirements. It logically follows, and the practice is, that these higher treatments will be met with CCA. Consider bridge decking. The minimum size that would be expected is 200x125 and the amount of sapwood on a piece of timber that size will be well under the 20% permitted loss as shown in Table 1 which is deemed to be acceptable under AS2082.[89] Further, all bridge decking is supplied against very tight species specifications written by the various main roads authorities. These species are all Durability Class 1 Above Ground Timbers, i.e. the heartwood automatically is equivalent to H5 treated or untreated.[90] H3 (above ground structural) is an adequate treatment for the non-structural amount of sapwood. The more so when it is considered that the sapwood will be protected by a bitumen running strip. Further, when the timber eventually is removed from service[91] the unnecessary presence of CCA should preclude its use in recycling. This product, along with wharf decking (for the same reasons) should be nominated as H3 but with a footnote saying, "when used in conjunction with the relevant State's Main Roads bridge timber specification".

The difference in requirement between a timber structure parallel to the coast, a wharf, and one perpendicular, a jetty eludes me, but they are considered different none the less. The requirements for hazard levels for jetty components (and frequently applied to boardwalk) which has remained unchanged since 2000, is H5 for fresh water and H6 for saltwater. As has been mentioned, it is impossible to achieve these levels in sawn timber through preservation with waterborne preservatives. With pre-drying and a high enough solution strength the sapwood certainly can reach H5, but it would be uncommon for the heartwood to be no more than 20%. Fortunately, as with bridge decking, H5 equivalence is automatic when appropriate timbers are used e.g., relying on a main roads' specification. Unfortunately, trying to explain to a non-timber person that an ironbark or spotted gum joist is equivalent to H5 when its sapwood at less than 20% of the cross section is treated to H3 is a frustrating, if not impossible, task[92].

---

[88] AS1604.1-2012, Table D1.

[89] This 20% figure is recognised as not being structurally important in clause 6.2 (b) (i) (B).

[90] AS 1604.1-2012, 5.2 (a).

[91] Premature bridge failure is, invariably, not because of treatment to H3 instead of H5. Rather inappropriate building practices are usually the issue e.g. the use of decking spikes and vertical rather than horizontal bolts. No amount of treatment will make up for this.

[92] The design life of a spotted gum joist treated to H3 in South East Queensland as determined by the *Timberlife* software, is 85 years, reflecting the adequacy of industry practice of treating to the lower level. Poor building practice will reduce this.

Figure 17. Turpentine bollard showing typical low quality of this species. The recycled timber in this project was reported to have shrunk 10% in a short period.

H6, or rather its equivalent, as mentioned can only be achieved in sawn timber through natural durability achieved and the only timber available is turpentine. The timber when unseasoned (Figure 17) is inappropriate[93] for use in jetties and structures due to its high shrinkage, high natural feature and lower resistance to impact forces.[94] So, ultimately a sawn H6 application is inappropriate. These products also should be treated to H3 in accordance with industry recommendations but qualified with a note about species selection as mentioned above.

Another area that needs clarification is the reference to being "occasionally submerged" in saltwater. Does an extreme but short-lived tide every couple of years come under this description? I have found that these words are being interpreted to such extremes.

My grave concern is that, if the Hazard Classification table is not corrected, designers will continue to rely on specifying unachievable H levels instead of designing appropriately. Fine points of detail in the selection of species, design e.g., dampcourses, and construction will be of far more importance than the introduction of CCA.

Why Treat Sawn Timber?
If waterborne treatments are not going to "preserve" sawn timber, just stabilise the sapwood, and if the amount of untreated sapwood, at least in hardwood 75 mm wide, is usually insufficient to make the timber non-structural, then why treat it at all? There are a number of reasons for doing so.

Hardwood

Figure 18. Untreated external floor joist

For non lyctus-susceptible timbers,[95] the issue of why we treat is generally not structural, particularly with thicker members. But it can be a very serious issue indeed. Under the requirements of AS2082 there is only a requirement to treat lyctus susceptible sapwood when it exceeds 20% of the cross section. The member in Figure 19 would be close to complying, if not actually complying with AS 2082. By contrast, there is no requirement to treat non lyctus susceptible timber even if it makes up 100% of the cross section Imagine the blackbutt member in Figure 18 where the sapwood, now decayed, at

---

[93] Timber Queensland, *Technical Data Sheet 7*, March 2006, Page 1. See further reference to turpentine under H6 marine.
[94] Bootle. *Wood...*, 345.
[95] AS 2982 lists the lyctus susceptibility of commonly used hardwood species in tables A1-A3.

the end was sitting in a joist hanger: it would have detached from the house. All external timber should be treated regardless of what is written in the codes.

Had that same piece of blackbutt been used internally as an exposed ceiling beam, and even with a high proportion of sapwood, it will exhibit no degrade of the sapwood and does not require any treating. Perception and expectation are important reasons for treating external timbers. There is expectancy among many purchasers that, if these timbers are not coloured by the treatment chemical, they are simply unfit for purpose. For commercial decking, the stabilisation of the sapwood is important because, if it decays, trip hazards are likely to occur. The lighter domestic decking may, in places, be virtually all sapwood, so treatment is critical.

Lyctus attack in roof truss

Lyctus attack in roof member

Figure 19. Lyctus attack

Figure 20. Lyctus larvae.

The situation with Lyctus susceptible timbers such as spotted gum and tallowwood is very different. These timbers have higher levels of starch in the sapwood. The lyctus beetle (Figure 20), sometimes called the powder post beetle for good reason, lays its eggs in the sapwood and its larvae will eat the sapwood and literally turn it to powder. This is nothing short of a nightmare inside a house, especially so when it occurs with decorative items such as polished flooring.

We have found that there is an expectation that timber can be supplied without sapwood. Our observation of the ex. 38 and 50mm decking we ran is that perhaps one piece in three contains significant amounts of sapwood. To supply sapwood free timber, in effect, means that much of a very limited resource is wasted and this is poor stewardship. Very few of the ex. 75mm joists and bearers would be totally free of sapwood.

While treatment kills any active larvae in the timber, it does not kill the eggs! The beetle can emerge in time leaving sometimes just a small pinhole but more often tracking in the timber. This can be a nuisance but is not structural if the sapwood is limited (Figure 21). The structural effect is similar to the effect of cylindrical auger beetle attack shown in the section *Preservatives Are Not Insect Repellents*. The treatment does however prevent further attack.

Pine

The philosophy behind pine treatment is exactly the opposite to that of hardwood. With hardwood, we start with a large portion of untreatable but durable heartwood and we need to preserve the lesser and usually, because of its small percentage, non-structural sapwood. With pine, we have a small portion of heartwood[96] which is untreatable, and we must preserve the structural non-durable sapwood. This takes treatment from being something that is frequently no more than cosmetic to something that is critical - preservation in the true sense of the word.

Figure 21. Emergent attack in treated timber by lyctus.

Figure 22. Untreated heart in pine extending to the outside surface.

Figure 23. Heart has decayed leaving outer treated sapwood.

Pine has exactly the same issues as hardwood. The outer sapwood band treats well and easily but it is very difficult to treat the heart. Figure 22 (again sprayed with a copper indicator), shows the untreated heart in a pine bollard. This bollard has been incised, that is, it has gone through a machine that puts thousands of small slits or pockets in the face. These pockets fill with chemical and allow penetration into the heartwood (sort of). The unavoidable consequence of not treating the heart is seen in Figure 23. Notice the decay is circular around the inside of the treatment. When the timber is being used as a post, it is possible to only incise the end that goes in the ground which would be H4 or H5 depending on the application and the top be left un-incised as it is only H3 unless for some reason the timber

Figure 24. Post with incised end is installed upside down

---

[96] The untreatable heart is not meant to exceed 20% of the cross section for H2-H6 e.g. AS1604.1-2011 5.2 (b) (i) (A). Frequently though heartwood is more than 20%.

remains moist.

Figure 25. Incised pine but only 3 mm deep.

When I tried to introduce a low-priced treated pine bollard instead of hardwood, I discussed our intention with the DPI Forestry which confirmed our opinion. To comply with the requirements of TUMA we would have to use incised pine. I purchased a trailer load, treated it and sent the samples for analysis for registering our plant for H4 pine. A full third of the samples failed because of poor penetration. I re-treated them and retested them. Again, they failed. I checked our process with the pine supplier. Yes, it was similar to theirs, but then they mentioned they only incised to a depth of 3mm and 3mm was the penetration in the failed samples, not 10mm. I could not sell the product legally and auctioned the load off at a substantial loss. It begs the question about the quality of the treatment of the H4 treated pine that is sold un-incised.

I was not deterred by this and decided to try again but I could not find one pine supplier in Australia that would supply me with the pine I needed. The problem was that we advised them that we would be sending the timber on to a laboratory for testing to confirm the 10mm penetration.

How did the situation of inadequately treated large section sawn pine arise? Treatment plants under TUMA (in Queensland) had to be registered to treat to a given hazard level[97] with a separate licence for the same H level in pine and hardwood. To obtain this registration and to be allowed to sell their treated product, the plant operator had to be able to prove that they could treat to a given chemical retention. Samples of product were submitted for analysis and inspection of penetration. In practice, it is relatively easy to achieve this in natural rounds so testing was done with them. However, that same licence also allowed the operator to treat sawn timber to the same H level. As most timber is used in H3 or lower applications there was often enough penetration to work satisfactorily. In H4 and H5 situations, the failure to gain enough penetration is likely to lead to failure. An example of the difficulty in purchasing a reliable structural member in pine was the Ironwood produced initially by Carter Holt Harvey.[98] Their treated and incised H4 pine was not suitable for structural applications.[99]

Figure 26. Incising round posts

---

[97] Part 4. Preservative treatment of timber, Section 19. Authorisation to use preservative treatment and registration of brand.
[98] This division was sold to AKD Softeoods in 2018. At the time of writing the brochures and website were not updated
[99] Despite the description page on Carter Harvey Holt's former website saying Ironwood is "Not suitable for structural applications e.g. structural retaining walls", another of their brochures IRONwood Garden Walls shows the product being used structurally!

Why H3 and not H5 for Extra Protection
We have often encountered situations where above ground applications (H3) are nominated to be treated to in-ground levels (H5). Surely, we should be reducing our chemical usage whenever possible and one way we can do this is by only using sufficient chemical. But how much is sufficient? Isn't it better to over treat and be certain? The amount of chemical needed to reach different levels was determined through establishing graveyard plots, in various locations around Australia, of timber treated with different levels of chemicals. The amount of decay was measured over an extended period of time. In above-ground applications, the decay hazard is lower so there is no need for extra chemical in the sapwood.

Figure 27.   Graveyard trial to test efficacy of treatment.

Over treatment through over specification also involves increased and unnecessary cost. This table shows the theoretical cost of chemicals for different hazard levels. These 2020 prices are before the treater adds profit and any additional labour. Some require post-dying and others pre-drying as well.

Chemical	Hardwood			Softwood		
	H3	H4	H5	H3	H4	H5
CCA	$5.50	$10.00	$17.00	$19.00	$31.50	$49.50
Azole based	$11.50	$25.00	$53.50	$39.50	$72.00	$131.00
ACQ	$15.50	$38.50	$66.00	$48.00	$122.00	$193.00
LOSP	??	N/A	N/A	$84.00	N/A	N/A
Table 5.	Treatment Costs/m^3. [100]					

Ultimately, the APVMA requires that the treatment chemicals be used in accordance with the manufacturer's instructions.

---

[100] The figures were supplied to the author by an industry source. The assumptions are: for hardwood, there is 15% sapwood, 10% safety figure, for pine, sapwood 100%, safety figure 10%..

H6 Marine

Figure 28. End attack of pile off-cut after 11 years on seabed.

Figure 29. Envelope protection broken by notch and bolt.

The General section that introduces the requirement for H6 under AS1604.1 2012 repeats the phrase "experience has shown" five times.[101] Presumably, this is a tactful way of saying that a lot of what passed for preservation simply did not work. I have been guilty of supplying piles double treated with CCA when that was permitted under Standards. It proved to be a fruitless though costly effort.

Envelope protection of natural rounds with a double treatment of CCA and pigment emulsified creosote has proven extraordinarily successful in marine piles. The image in Figure 28 was taken at Baker's Marina in Pittwater, NSW. When the original marina was built in 1968 turpentine piles were used. When the marina was extended in 1972 the owners used Koppers double treated marine piles, the off-cuts from the piles simply dropped in the water.[102] During inspections of the piles in 1982 a diver was sent down to recover some off-cuts. Toredo had heavily attacked the heartwood as it was exposed at both ends but did not touch the H6 envelope. So, if the pile is embedded deeply and the top is above the high tide mark there should be no serious attack over its service life. This 1982 inspection reported the condition of the piles at low tide being "as new". At reinspection in 1993 the turpentine piles were badly damaged, but the double treated marine piles were still as new. In 1998, three of the piles were removed to temporarily modify mooring facilities for a large vessel and after 26 years the same piles were reinstated when the vessel left![103]

Actual life expectancy will vary dramatically throughout Australia as hazards vary considerably. The application could involve direct exposure to the ocean, or in a more sheltered area such as a marina or on a tidal river which is less severe still. Marine organisms are more aggressive in warmer water so an application in Cairns will have a much shorter life than one in Sydney. This is, after all, the most aggressive environment that timber is likely to be used in. Whatever the environment, a longer life expectancy can be achieved over simply using turpentine piles.

---

[101] Clause 7.1

[102] This should not be done as PEC can bleed from the end grain of the timber and produce a very thin oil slick, Koppers Wood Products Pty. Ltd. *Treated Hardwood Marine Piles Case Studies Revision 0*, 2009, 4.

[103] Koppers. *Treated ...*, 4.

Invariably premature failures are attributable to bad specification and building practice, not the product itself as shown in Figure 29 where we see a marine pile from near Kiama that is failing. Firstly, it failed because it had the wrong treatment. It was CCA-treated which is not allowed north of Bateman's Bay in NSW. Even if treated correctly, it would still have failed as the sapwood was notched and drilled in the tidal zone. The answer is to use a bigger pile that does not need bracing where there can be attack. Figure 30 shows marine attack on a pile treated with CCA only from the Gold Coast. It is evident that the CCA has offered no worthwhile protection against marine borers. It was later reused as a bridge girder by someone in a misguided attempt at economy.

Figure 30. Marine attack of CCA treated timber on the Gold Coast.

As for sawn timber, again it cannot be treated to H6 because you cannot achieve an envelope protection. You must rely on natural durability. The only commercially available[104] Australian timber with the highest level of natural durability in a marine application is turpentine. On drying, it shrinks 12%, has lower resistance to impact forces, splits, collapses, has a lot of natural feature and, in general, is a very undesirable timber. (It is, however, a good decking when kiln dried and carefully graded).[105] Specifying sawn timber for a true H6 application, in our opinion, is not a wise option. Pine sapwood will receive the chemical, but the knot cluster cannot be treated which can be attacked by marine organisms[106] giving structural issues. The superstructures of marinas and decks are only a H3 application. This view is in keeping with industry technical publications and guides.[107]

This claim, however, is contrary to AS 1604.1-2000, through to 2012 Table D1 which asked for H5 Treatment above fresh water and H6 above saltwater for jetties (other than decking). Are these Standards incorrect? Jack Norton, former Programme Leader - Timber Protection Programme of Horticulture and Forestry Science Division, Department of Primary Industries and Fisheries (who was responsible for administering the treatment provisions of TUMA in Queensland) said:

> "In response to your questions about the most appropriate hazard class for jetty components, I propose to have the matter raised at the next meeting of Australian Standards Committee TM6. In my opinion, timber that is exposed out of ground subject to periodic moderate wetting and leaching is subject to a Hazard Class H3 exposure. In Table D1 of Australian Standard AS1604.1, jetty components are listed as being exposed to a H5 (fresh water) or a H6 (salt water) Hazard. I believe that the intention here is for material that comes in contact with the

---

[104] AS5064-2005 also lists satinay and belian. Satinay has very limited availability but Timber Queensland advised was available near the North Coast, Coolola areas. Belian is imported.
[105] Timber Queensland. *Technical Data Sheet 7*, March 2006, 1.
[106] Nguyen, Minh N, Robert H. Leicester, and Chi-hsiang Wang. Manual 7 – Marine borer attack on timber structures. (Melbourne: FWPA. 2008) 11. The Manual suggests the knot cluster can be protected by a copper band but it needs regular maintenance.
[107] E.g. Timber Queensland. *Technical Data Sheet 7*, March 2006, 1.

water through immersion or tidal action. In my opinion, material above the water should be considered to be a H3 exposure hazard; however I will raise the matter at the Standards Committee with a view to reviewing the current classification."

Examples of Marine Durability	
Species	Class
spotted gum	4
blackbutt	3
red ironbark	2
turpentine	1
Table 6. From AS5604-2005 Table A1.	

Similar advice was received from another committee member, Colin McKenzie, Manager, Timber Applications and Use with Timber Queensland. The Standard had to be read with common sense. The foundations which are in constant contact with water are the only part that must be H5 or H6. H6 through chemical means on sawn hardwood is unachievable in every Australian grown sawn hardwood as penetration of 20mm is required for marine durability 2 to 4 species. No penetration is required for marine durability 1.[108]

Natural pine rounds are generally considered unsuitable for H6 treatment. The timber actually treats very well but the knot cluster, as mentioned in the discussion on sawn timber, is untreatable and can be attacked by marine organisms.[109] This is unfortunate as there are situations where the light weight and uniform size of the pine posts are very desirable. Such an application is a boardwalk foundation in a mangrove environment. A practice we have found satisfactory is to treat to H5 and add a physical barrier to prevent attack. This is a long-standing effective practice.

Figure 31. H5 posts with addition of sleeves for a marine application.

Figure 32. Untreated but sleeved ironbark

Figure 33. Grouted ironbark pile from

---

[108] Analysis of 200x200 untreated (i.e. free of sap but coloured by the treatment) turpentine and ironbark with the *Timberlife* software shows 50% residual bending strength after 15 years and 5 years respectively. A 200mm double treated marine pile using a marine durability 2 natural round with 25mm envelope of sapwood is 45 years by contrast. The figures are based on Brisbane.

[109] AS 1601.1-2010 says in Table H6.2 that pine is suitable when double treated but we disagree due to the effect of the knot cluster.

piles installed at Picnic Bay Jetty, Magnetic Island. Installed 1959. Magnetic Island is in sound condition.

Physical barriers can be so effective in preventing marine attack that they challenge the life expectancy (but not the simplicity) of H6 treated marine piles. The piles salvaged from the Picnic Bay jetty at Magnetic Island (off Townsville) revealed that after fifty years in this environment the condition of the ironbark piles with this form of protection is very good. It was reported that even in ungrouted areas there was very little attack as well'[110] It must be remembered that marine attack is more active in tropical waters which makes this result all the more remarkable.

A Word of Caution

The legal requirement of where CCA can be used in the attachment does not apply to imported treated timber which is totally exempt from the requirements of the APVMA. Be very careful what you are purchasing. Remember also that the levels of chemical can also be much lower. Table 7 shows a comparison between standards is based on timber of 850 kg/m3.

Use in Malaysia	Malaysia Kg/m3 Salts	Malaysia % m/m Oxide	U.K. % m/m Oxide	Australia % m/m Oxide	Application Australia	Example
C5	8	.47	.6	.6	H3	decking
C4	12	.7	1.0	1.0	H4	sleepers
C3/C2	16	.94	1.0	1.6	H5	poles
C1	32	1.87	1.7	Not permitted above Perth latitude	H6	Marine piles
Table 7.	Different international treatment standards.					

---

[110] Kochanek, Simon. *Pers. Com.* November 28, 2011. Mr. Kochanek is Principal Structural Engineer of Bligh Tanner Consulting Engineers.

5 BRANDING AND IDENTIFICATION

Branding

The treatment brand consists of three groups of numbers and letters, e.g. 049 70 H2. The first three numbers identify the treatment plant, the second set refers to the treatment chemical used (70 is for permethrin) and the last two are the hazard level to which the sapwood is protected. For many years, I have viewed the branding of sawn hardwood as an exercise in futility at best, misleading at worst! By contrast, with VPI treated sawn pine, incised to the correct depth, branding is meaningful and should be accurate.

Figure 34. Pole identification disk.

The only meaningful branding of hardwood I have seen is the identification system used on power poles, a product which has protected sapwood surrounding unprotected heartwood (envelope protection). The production of power poles is tightly controlled with full documentation by the producer, especially of the species, from the forest to sale and then monitored by the power authority from installation to the end of its service life. At a nominated height above ground, a disc is inserted with the manufacturer's pole number, species, size and other information as required under the individual specification. That disc may be secured by a nail and remains with the pole its entire life.

By contrast, consider sawn hardwood, a brand is attached or stamped in the end that says, say, H3. Most purchasers do not understand that that refers only to the sapwood which, I have argued, for most pieces is well within the 20% want and wane limits, meaning failure of the treatment is not going to affect the structural integrity should the sapwood decay. The remaining heartwood, if produced in Queensland, is usually at least a Durability 2 In-Ground species making the timber equal to a H5 piece of timber according to the letter of the Standard (but not necessarily in reality). The example of a treated, then dressed piece of blackbutt has been given. The branding in these cases can either underrepresent or overrepresent the durability of the timber. The branded end is then cut off and disposed of and with that any record of the treatment plant and hazard level is lost. There was no provision under TUMA to supply a certificate which, at least, has a chance to get into the file and provide a permanent record. Despite that, specifications should require that a certificate of treatment be supplied.

My concern with branding is that it can engender a sense of false security. Few purchasers associate the brand with just the sapwood but consider that it reflects the whole, even when the piece may contain no sapwood. At times, branding could not be further from the truth. Some years ago, our family was selling a small country sawmill we owned. The purchaser was a sawmill that only cut landscaping timber. We explained that the forestry allocation we had at the time was in an area which was predominantly rose gum. Rose gum is a Durability 3 In Ground timber with a small sapwood band and most definitely is not suitable for ground contact. "No worries", was the reply, "We will just take it to the treatment plant, and they will stamp it H5". Where does responsibility lie, with the sawmill or with the treater? Under TUMA it lay completely with the treater, but consider his dilemma, sawn rose gum looks just like forest red gum which is Durability 1 In Ground. Strictly, material should not be presented to treatment plants that cannot be easily identified and treated.

With the repeal of TUMA it was not clear for Queenslanders, and for other States that do not have a similar Act, what the actual requirements, (as opposed to common practice), were for branding. There was no mechanism within those States to register treatment plants to generate the first three numbers of the brand. The BCA was probably out of step with the complementary Acts or lack thereof. Many items do not even come under the BCA, e.g. agricultural applications, while some items are sold as products, not as treated pieces of timber. The insistence by NSW Forestry on all timber coming into the State being branded with a number of a plant registered by that State, though not necessarily situated there, could possibly even have be construed as a "restraint of trade across borders". Clarity finally came after NSW repealed its TMA in 2013 and responsibility for issuing the brands came under the responsibility of the Timber Preservers Association of Australia.

Figure 35. Poor branding (or no branding) of H3 LOSP treated LVL in a deck in Brisbane.

The branding of LVL is a vexing issue for which there does not seem to be a practical answer. Consider the application in Figure 35, from an inspection I undertook in 2018, which typifies bad building practice with LVL used in decks. The joists were not painted, not end sealed and had no sealing strip on top of the joists. This bears no relation to any LVL manufacturers recommendations and that is enough to ensure that the structure will fail prematurely but as no fault of the manufacturer or treatment. But was the product itself ever suitable for this application as it is either totally unbranded or branded as H2S, for internal use south of the Tropic of Capricorn. Most of them however (though not all) have a green tinge suggesting a post treatment to H3 but without any rebranding it must remain speculation.

On a practical level, the LVL manufacturers generally do not have a timber treatment plant, and unless they have used glueline preservative it is produced and stored as an untreated and unbranded product. Others import a quantity of or all their LVL treated to H2S and may be branded full length. This untreated (or H2S) material is stored in a distribution warehouse system until an order for H2S, H2 or H3 comes in at which point the untreated or H2S LVL is then assembled into an order and sent off for post manufacturing treatment with instructions to treat the product to a required level. Invariably this is to an

LOSP treatment plant as the process is fast, generally has low uptakes and the treated product is not degraded through the expansion caused by water based high absorption treatments. A detriment is that LOSP treatments were originally designed for window components which were for treated in their final shape and form giving end grain penetration and not in multiple or untrimmed lengths. This makes them subject to what I consider the misuse highlighted in Figure 35.

Compliance with the treatment Standards require that the timber is branded with the plant and preservative identification and the hazard class. The LVL product could be branded along its length but to do this the bundle would have to be broken down, branded, and then repacked. Instead, this brand is often on the end which is the first thing that is cut off on site though it can also be removed during processing or construction, then the piece, by definition, becomes non-compliant even if it is properly treated. (This applies to all treated products not just LVL.) The process is an envelope the specified envelope penetration for H3 for example, is 15 mm from the surface, 20 mm from the edges and 150 mm from the ends) which means it does not necessarily penetrate to the core of the LVL should it be over 40 mm thick which, invariably, it is when being used as joists.

For their part, the treatment plant generally produces compliant product through processing correctly and correctly adding end tags to all the pieces in a freshly treated pack. This means that, in the majority of cases, the product leaves the treatment plant correctly treated and branded. This material then gets shipped to site or to a manufacturing facility where the correctly treated product is docked into usable lengths. This docked product becomes non-compliant:

- Because the brand has been removed and, more importantly
- Envelope penetration patterns for envelope treated timber may have been breached.

Finally, for H2/3&4 treated product, the standard states that "All envelope-treated laminated veneer lumber (LVL) shall carry a warning that suitable remedial treatment (such as an appropriate brush-on preservative) shall be applied to all fresh-cut surfaces".[111] This is an area where much more needs to be done to enforce (or reinforce) this requirement to both the producers and the specifiers/users.[112] If there is any doubt, those responsible for signing off a structure where visible branding does not match the application should be prepared to have independent sampling undertaken.

---

[111] AS1604.4 7.4. confirm
[112] For this section on branding of LVL I am indebted to Jack Norton *Pers Com*. September 26, 2020.

6 PRESERVATION AND CORROSION

Factors Affecting Corrosion

The obvious part of the testing regime for registration of a preservative that applied when TUMA was in force was to determine if the compound did actually penetrate the sapwood. But equally important was the need to determine if the preservative corrodes fasteners or even the treatment plant itself. Obviously, fasteners must be as durable as the timber. Over the history of preservation research, otherwise effective treatments have been rejected because of corrosion problems.[113]

In a sealed, dry roof space or other application where the timber is not exposed to a marine environment or pollutants, the impact of preservation and resultant choice of bolt type is largely irrelevant. The Timberlife design life prediction software indicates that minimum corrosion will occur in galvanised bolts. This is an ideal application which historically was served well even by black steel bolts and nails where life expectancy can be measured in hundreds of years.[114] Move away from these ideal circumstances and there is a wide divergence of opinion as to when to use galvanised or stainless. Unfortunately, clear direction for additional corrosion resistance for fasteners, nailplates and strapping for different environments is not given in the NCC (formerly the BCA) or The Residential Timber-framed Construction Standard, AS1684-2010 series. The Standard specifies in Clause 1.15 that "all metal used in structural timber connections shall be provided with corrosion protection appropriate for the particular conditions". With clauses like "level of corrosion protection shall take into consideration", the responsibility for choosing the correct corrosion resistance was passed to the specifier.[115] Considering especially the effect of preservation, what then might these guidelines be?

When writing the earlier edition of this guide, I asked one preservative manufacturer for their guidelines on where to use stainless and where to use galvanised bolts. They referred the matter to the lawyers in the United States who replied that we need to follow bolt manufacturers' recommendations. I then tried to find a bolt manufacturer that had a recommendation for use with treated timber and they simply did not exist. In the face of, in some cases, a deliberate omission of recommendations, to in other cases, readily available but conflicting or less complete guidelines,[116] the correct decision of when to it is appropriate to use stainless bolts over the less expensive galvanised in treated timber can be difficult. On top of this, the specifier must deal with customers who object to and can even aggressively oppose any cost increase that may result from nominating stainless.

Weather exposure is the complicating factor in the choice of a fastener for treated timber. Should a joint be protected from the weather such as trusses in a non-ventilated roof space, the matter is quite

---

[113] Davis, Robin I. *Timber Preservatives and Corrosion*, International Research Group on Wood Preservation, Working Group III, Preservatives and Method of Treatment. (Document IRG/WP/3228) Prepared for the 14th annual meeting Gold Coast, 1983.

[114] Zelinka, Samuel. Corrosion of Metals in Wood Products in *Developments in Corrosion Protection*, Editor M Aliofkhazraei (InTech, 2014), 584.

[115] Pryda. *Technical Update Corrosion Resistance of Pryda Products* Feb. 2012, 1. URL: http://www.pryda.com.au/wp-content/uploads/2016/05/Post-Anchor-Guide-March-2012.pdf. Date accessed: 15 December 2016.

[116] At the time of writing, there is considerable difference between recommendations from the Timber Preservers Association of Australia, Arch Wood Protection, Koppers Performance Chemicals and Timber Queensland,

straightforward. Correctly galvanised fasteners have proven satisfactory as the moisture content of the timber quickly drops to below 20% so decay is not an issue and as there is no ongoing wetting and drying of the timber corrosion, as will be explained, is not an issue. To come to a conclusion about which material to use externally, it is helpful to take into consideration the other factors that can impact on corrosion other than treatment and these are:
- pH of the timber
- The moisture content of the timber
- Environmental considerations
- The presence of decay
- Fastener quality

PH of the Timber

Species	pH	Trouble
Blackbutt	3.6	yes
Mountain ash	4.7	no
Ironbark, red narrow leaf	4.0	yes
Spotted gum	4.5	no
Rose gum	5.1	no
Jarrah	3.3	yes
Radiata	4.8	no
Table 8. Corrosion from acidity of timber.[117]		

If the joint is to be exposed to any moisture, the acidity of the timber must be considered. Corrosion can be an issue when the Ph drops below 4.3. While the pH of a piece of timber varies within the piece and from piece to piece there are published values which can be used as a guide (Refer Table 8) If the specification is just, say, "F14" it has to be assumed that a species with a lower pH will be supplied. By nominating a species outside of the problem range, such as spotted gum, the consequences of corrosion can be minimised.

Moisture Content of the Timber

Given the relatively benign chemistry of wood it can appear a simple environment where corrosion is not a challenge but wood "has a complex interaction with water that greatly affects its physical and chemical properties including corrosion."[118] Wood is a hydrophilic material meaning it has a strong affinity with water and some species can absorb up to 200% of their dry mass as water. This water can be either free liquid water or water vapour in the cells and cavities or bound water held by intermolecular forces in the cell walls. The point where the free water is expelled, and only bound water is present is called the fibre saturation point and is normally about 30% moisture content. In service, moisture is given off and taken in freely until it reaches equilibrium with its environment.[119] Below a moisture content of 15-18% embedded fasteners do not corrode but will start to increase around 20% and reach a maximum corrosion rate at or above fibre saturation point.[120] The implications are that there are applications for fasteners that present no challenge from timber moisture such as roof trusses made from kiln dried pine and others which are very difficult such as a pergola in a tropical region which is being continually wet.

---

[117] This table is drawn from Bootle, Keith R. *Wood in Australia, Types, properties and uses, Second Edition*. (North Ryde: McGraw Hill Australia, 2005), 60-1 and Table 2.3.3 of Forests and Wood Products Australia. *Manual 6 – Embedded corrosion of fasteners in exposed timber structures*. (Melbourne. Forest and Wood Products Australia: 2007). On this scale a pH of 0 is highly acidic, 7 is neutral and 14 is highly alkaline. The scale is logarithmic with a 10 fold jump between each unit.
[118] Zelinka. *Corrosion ...*, 568.
[119] Zelinka. *Corrosion ...*, 568.
[120] Zelinka. *Corrosion ...*, 574.

Environmental Considerations

Figure 36.　　Sons of Gwalia headrig.

A further factor that will influence the choice of fasteners is the climate. The Australian climate is very varied, from hot humid tropics to dry deserts. The heritage listed headrig from the Sons of Gwalia mine at Gwalia (a two hour drive north of Kalgoorlie) in Western Australia in the Great Victoria Desert was built during 1886-8 from 300x300 Oregon pine. About a third has been replaced with kauri which is not a great deal more durable (In Ground Durability 3) but basically the timber has lasted ten times longer than you would normally expect. The bolts are just black steel without any corrosion protection and they, just like the timber, have survived because there is seldom any moisture. Invariably, designers will have to deal with the effects of a more aggressive environment.

The embedded corrosion hazard zone map in Figure 36 shows Australia broken up into three zones. These zones are determined by the mean annual surface equilibrium moisture content ($SEMC_{mean}$). The boundaries for these are C the highest risk 15%, B a medium risk at 12% and A, the lowest and where Gwalia is found, 9%. To this climate map the designer has to factor into his assessment the impact of marine exposure (less than 1 km from the coast) and, further, whether the products being joined are sheltered from the rain, and if not, is it a vertical or a horizontal surface.[122] This means there is a large variation in risk due to environmental considerations alone.

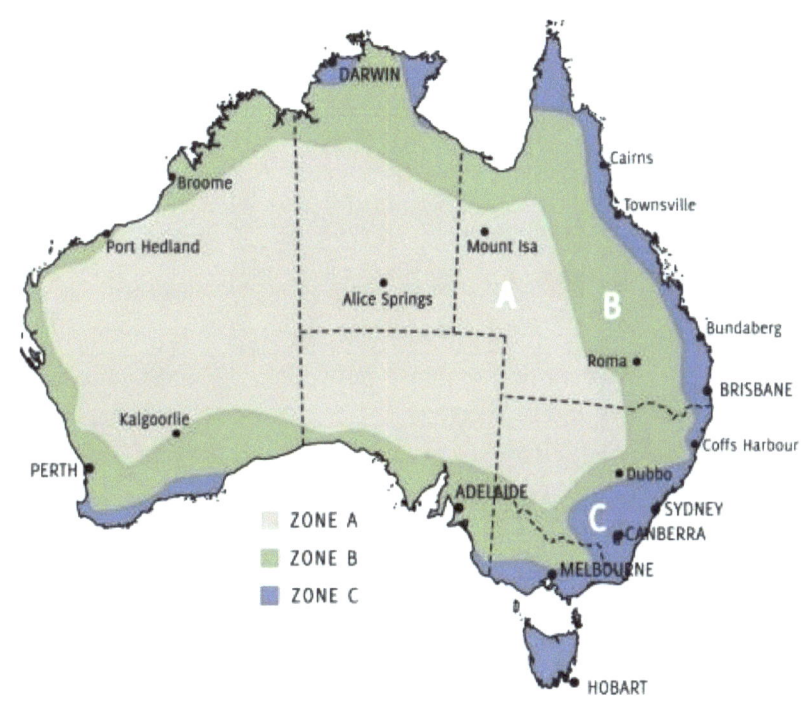

Figure 37.　　Embedded corrosion hazard zone map.[121]

Fastener Quality

The galvanising process is far from novel as it was first patented in 1837 and its effectiveness was recognised to such an the extent that by as early as 1850 the British galvanising industry was using 10,000 tonne of zinc a year to protect steel. But what is not often appreciated is the difference between atmospheric corrosion of galvanised fasteners as we would see in, say, a steel bridge and corrosion of the

---

[121] FWPA. *Manual 6 ...*, 7
[122] FWPA. *Manual 6 ...*, 6-8

same fasteners in timber. Because the coating works well in the one application it was assumed that it will perform equally well in others and this has not proven to be a safe assumption.[123] In the case of atmospheric corrosion of zinc, specific oxides form (hydrozincite and smithsonite) on the surface and protect the zinc from further corrosion. When installed in timber, different oxides form (namuwite, simonkolleite and sometimes hydrozincite) which do not give the protection layer seen with atmospheric corrosion. Without this passivating layer, wood corrosion on galvanised fasteners can even be faster than non-galvanised steel fasteners.[124] To complicate matters, under different exposure conditions galvanised fasteners have been shown to corrode more slowly than steel.[125]

A further factor to consider when choosing galvanised or stainless is the deteriorating quality of many if not most imported galvanised bolts. Careful specification of the bolt coating thickness, while important, is ultimately meaningless if it is not backed up regular testing of grade compliance.[126] At the time of writing there has started to be some regulatory awareness of this problem as corrosion has been reported in hold down bolts in houses, an application which is sheltered from the weather.

Figure 38.   Different performance between galvanised fastener and bracket.

But before discussing this, consider first a well-made and well galvanised bolt. It is important to understand that even this bolt does not have the same longevity as galvanised steel rod of the same thickness. Bolts are galvanised in small batches in wire cages which are then spun at high revolutions to remove excess zinc and give a clean thread. The typical minimum coating thickness for a 10 mm bolt or larger would be 390 g/m^2 or 55 microns. By contrast, the minimum coated thickness for steel over 6 mm, which sits in the vat for up to 10 minutes is 600 g/m^2 or 85 microns and regularly reaches 700-900 g/m^2. Longevity is dependent on the zinc coating so normal steel could have an expected life of 30 to 50% longer than that of the bolt.[127] This can be seen in Figure 38 where the bolt heads are corroding and the hot dipped bracket is sound. But that is assuming that the bolt is of high quality and that does not necessary follow. Now that cup head and general use hexagon head bolts being imported to Australia, it is an industry observation that the life expectancy of the galvanised finish has deteriorated dramatically.

---

[123] Zelinka. *Corrosion* ..., 587.
[124] Zelinka. *Corrosion* ..., 574-5. See also Zelinka, Samuel, Rebecca Sichel, Donald Stone. Exposure testing of fasteners in preservative treated wood: Galvimetric corrosion rates and corrosion product analysis in *Corrosion Science* 52 (2010) 3947 where it is reported that several researchers have observed that zinc corrosion protected products can corrode more rapidly.
[125] Zelinka. *Exposure* ..., 3947.
[126] I am aware that ITW Proline do this, but smaller importers may not.
[127] Robinson, John. *Specifiers Manual.* (Carole Park: Industrial Galvanisers, 2013), 15.

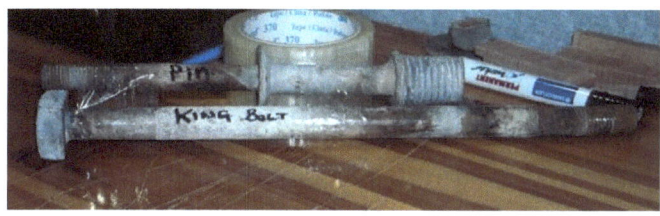

Figure 39.   Australian made galvanised bolt after 50 years' service in Millmerran, Qld. Bolts were removed in 2001.

Figure 40.   Imported galvanised bolt after 12 months in Gatton, Qld c. 2003.

While poor performance of many galvanised fasteners is known among the industry, trying to find information in the public arena on the seriousness of the situation is very difficult. It is almost like a conspiracy of silence. The one article I could find based on tests conducted on four batches of bolts purchased from different manufacturers in China summarised the situation as follows "The anti-corrosion performance of the four hot-dip galvanizing bolts obtained from different companies were all unsatisfactory. The causes of the above phenomenon are the lower thickness of the hot-dip coating, too much defects on the surface of the coatings and the elemental composition impurity".[128] How great was the variability of the galvanising? The average coating thickness on individual bolts went from 130 micron[129] to 34 microns and the minimum was 13 microns which happened to be on the same bolt that averaged 130 microns. This is greater variability than timber and can mean that the bolt, not the timber, is the weak link in the system. Note that Industrial Galvanisers indicate that a well galvanised bolt should be 55 microns.

Preservative Used

Another factor that impacts upon corrosion when fasteners are weather exposed is the preservative used. Newer preservatives ACQ and Tanalith E (also called copper azole or CuAz) have proven effective replacements for CCA as far as timber decay is concerned. But without the chrome and arsenic, these alternative chemicals require a significantly higher level of copper in the timber than with CCA. A higher concentration of water soluble copper is "more likely to initiate serious corrosion of susceptible metallic components embedded in or in contact with these timbers".[130] Corrosion could be from four to nine times that of CCA over a one year period.[131] The iron and hydroxyl ions released from the corrosion attacks the cellulose components of the timber causing "nail sickness" whereby there is significant loss in the

---

[128] Li. Cuoxin, Shanjing Xia, Yilang Peng. Anti-Corrosion Performance of Four Hot Dip Galvanising Bolts in *Applied Mechanics and Materials Vols. 395-396* (2013), 708-71.

[129] The paper was expressed in um, there is one micron to one um.

[130] Li, Z.W., N.J. Marston and M.S. Jones. *Corrosion of Fasteners in Treated Timber* Study Report SR241 2011 (Branz, 2011), i

[131] Li. *Corrosion …*, i. Bootle initially corrosion was thought to more than double that of CCA. *Wood …, 62*. Simpson Strong-Tie after testing 2600 samples assessed them as a little more than double. Anon, *Preservative Treated Wood Technical Bulletin No. T-PRWOOD08-R* (Pleasanton: Simpson Strong-Tie,. 2008), 3. This assessment was based on accelerated weathering tests based on the American Wood-Preservers Association Standard E12-94 *Standard Method for Determining Corrosion of Metal in Contact with Treated Wood*.

structural integrity of the joint.[132] By contrast, it has been argued that the chrome and/or arsenic of CCA can have a passivating effect on fasteners.[133]

Fastener Recommendations

It is further helpful to consider manufacturers' and industry body recommendations and long term field trials. The Timber Preservers Association of Australia (TPAA) has a very simple recommendation for fasteners in CCA – "Hot dipped galvanised nails, bolts and coach screws should be used in corrosive environments, e.g. swimming pool structures, marine structures, [and] in the immediate vicinity of the sea-coast, where air-borne salt spray represents a very severe hazard to metal fittings and fixings".[134] This is not in keeping with one of their members, Lonza's, recommendations. I view the TPAA guidelines as far from adequate and can lead to premature failure.[135]

There is no recommendation at the time of writing by TPAA for non-chrome, non-arsenic treatments. Two very useful guides for the Australian specifier are published by Timber Queensland and as mentioned, Lonza. Lonza Chemicals' publication for the Americas, *Corrosion and Hardware Recommendations for Treated Wood*[136], is the document used as the basis for recommendations by that company for Australia. It is reproduced in simplified form which removes information only relevant to North America.

---

[132] Li. *Corrosion …*, ii.
[133] Rammer, Douglas, Samuel Zelinka, Philip Line. *Fastener Corrosion: Testing, Research and Design Considerations* a paper given at World Conference on Timber Engineering 2006, 1.
[134] Timber Preservers Association of Australia *Fasteners in CCA Treated Timber*. URL: http://www.tpaa.com.au/fasteners-for-cca/. Date accessed: 5 October 2020.
[135] I am aware of a boardwalk in the Cairns region where galvanized bolts were used on the seafront and bolt replacement started after only six months.
[136] Arch Wood Protection, Inc. and Arch Treatment Technologies, Inc. *Hardware Recommendations for Treated Wood.* June 6, 2006. (No publication details), 2-3.

Recommendations for Copper Azole and CCA Treated Wood[1]					
Important Note: In severe environments having an unusually high corrosion hazard such as those that are continuously wet or within 5 miles (8 km) of salt water, in critical architectural applications where appearance is of great importance, and in structural applications of an especially critical nature or where an exceptionally long service life is required, the use of hardware having corrosion durability equivalent to or greater than 304 or 316 stainless steel should be used					
	Indoors always Dry (<15% MC)	Protected from weather Dampness OK	Outdoor in Weather - regular wetting	Coastal applications	Wood foundation & other critical applications
Fasteners	Mild Steel, EP(2), HDG, MG, Copper, 304/316 SS	HDG, MG, Copper, 304/316 SS	HDG, MG, Copper, 304/316 SS	304/316 SS	304/316 SS
Connectors, light gauge steel	HDG (3), Copper 304/316 SS	HDG, 304/316 SS	HDG, 304/316 SS	304/316 SS	NA
Connectors, heavy duty welded steel	HDG, 304/316 SS	HDG, 304/316 SS	HDG, 304/316 SS	304/316 SS	NA
Flashing (4)	Copper, 304/316 SS HDG (3)	Copper, 304/316 SS HDG	Copper, 304/316 SS HDG	304/316 SS	Copper, 304/316 SS
Table 9.	Corrosion protection with Copper Azole, and CCA.				

Borates & Dricon® Fire Retardant Treated Wood[1]		
	Indoors, Always Dry (<15% MC)	Protected, Can be damp for extended periods
Fasteners	Mild Steel, EP, HDG, MG, Aluminium, Copper, 304/316 SS	HDG, Aluminium, Copper, 304/316 SS
Connectors light gauge steel	EP, HDG, MG 304/316 SS	HDG. 304/316 SS
Connectors Heavy duty welded steel	HDG, MG 304/316 SS	HDG -ASTM A123 304/316 SS
Flashing	HDG, MG, Aluminum, Copper, 304/316 SS	HDG,MG, Aluminum, Copper, 304/316 SS
Table 10.	Corrosion protection with Borates and Fire retardant treatments.	

Notes to Tables:
(1) Key to Metals in Tables: HDG: Hot-dipped galvanised steel MG: Mechanically galvanized steel EP – Electroplated SS: Stainless Steel
(2) Arch regards the use of hot-dipped galvanised fasteners as preferable to using non-galvanised or electroplated steel nails, though these are regarded as acceptable when attaching framing to copper azole treated timbers if that wood has been dried after treatment and will remain dry in a H2 application. Their recommendations point out, but do not take issue with, the International Residential Code which allows non galvanised bolts when the diameter is ½" (12mm) and larger, even for foundation bolts. We would question the wisdom of this.
(3) Standard galvanised strapping is regarded as acceptable for fastening copper azole treated wood to foundations providing it is used in a H2 application.
(4) Aluminium in the presence of moisture is subject to dissimilar metal corrosion when in contact with either CCA or copper azole treated wood. "Aluminium should only be used in normally dry applications where a barrier can be installed that
(a) provides complete separation of the (without penetrating fasteners) from the treated wood and that,
(b) will remain intact for the service life of the flashing. Aluminium nails, screws, fasteners and connectors should not be used in wood treated with copper based preservatives".[137]

As far as fasteners with ACQ are concerned, I was not able to find thorough recommendations similar to those that were available from Lonza for their CCA alternatives. Koppers Performance Chemicals urge "compliance with building codes for the intended use" which, as has been shown, is very vague. Fastener recommendations for use with CCA [similarly for ACQ] products include hot dipped galvanised, stainless steel and other fasteners as recommended by the fastener manufacturer."[138] They also advise not using ACQ preserved wood in direct contact with aluminium. Considering the serious implications that can follow a fastener failure due to the effect of treatment, the difficulty with these recommendations are that "manufacturer's recommendations" simply are not readily available, if at all.[139] I am loathe to say it, but there seems little option other than to follow the guidelines of their competitor. As an order of non-chrome, non-arsenic treated timber is likely to contain either ACQ or Tanalith E, regardless of what is specified, it would have been useful to know if ACQ had extra corrosion resistance requirements to Tanalith E. Timber treated with ACQ is more corrosive than timber treated with Tanalith E.[140]

---

[137] Arch. *Fastener...*, 4.
[138] Koppers Performance Chemicals. *Naturwood ACQ*. 2006, 2. URL: http://www.kopperspc.com.au/pdf/micropro-brochure.pdf. Date accessed: 15 December 2016, and Koppers Performance Chemicals. *Lifewood CCA*. 2006, 2. URL: http://www.kopperspc.com.au/pdf/Lifewood-cca-brochure.pdf. date accessed: 15 December 2016.
[139] Dr Saman Fernando, Manager, Engineering Research Development and Innovation for Ajax Engineered Fasteners advised that Ajax did not have recommendations. *Pers. Com.* March 27, 2012.
[140] In all cases, the ACQ H3.2 [corrosion] values ... were approximately 1.5 to 3.8 times that measured for the CCA H3.2 timber ... and CuAz H3.2. Kear, G, Hai-Zhen Wu, Mark Jones . The *Corrosion of Metallic Fasteners in Untreated, CCA-, CuAz-, and ACQ-based timbers. Branz Study Report* 153. (Judgeford: Branz, 2006), 92.

Figure 41.   Z275 bracket used near a swimming pool.

The different nailplate manufacturers came to an agreed position on where to use stainless and where to use galvanised connectors in 2016. This is reflected in Timber Queensland's *Technical Data Sheet 35, Corrosion Resistance of Metal Connectors*. This guide identifies different corrosion zones:

- Sea spray zone (less than 1 km from a surf coast, 100 m from bayside areas)
- Coastal zone (1 – 10 km from surf coast, or 1 km from bayside)
- Industrial zone (close to complexes emitting corrosive gasses)
- Special Hazard (e.g. enclosed swimming pools where stainless may even corrode and beyond the scope of the data sheet)
- Low hazard zone (anywhere outside the four areas listed above)

This is then broken down into three exposure conditions

- Enclosed (within a closed roof, floor and wall cavity)
- Sheltered (subject to wind-blown salt but not washed with rain, e.g. open garages and sub-floors)
- Exposed (experiencing both weather and rain, e.g. decks and pergolas).

In all exposed allocations in the four areas covered by the guide, 316 grade stainless is required (or else specially prepared plates). For the sheltered applications, an area not differentiated by some recommendations prior to 2016, a standard Z275 (275 grammes of galvanising per m2 total both sides i.e. 138 gsm actual per side) can only be used in the Low Hazard Zone, other applications require either stainless (Seaspray Zone) or the addition of soft seal paint (Coastal and Industrial). Where there is little risk of corrosion such as in an enclosed and sealed roof area Z275 can be used even in a Seaspray Zone. Further, these recommendations are for non-treated timber and those treated with waterborne preservatives can require additional paint protection which for simplicity basically forces you to stainless.[141]

Further driving a specifier to stainless at least with the thin connectors is the difficulty in achieving 600 gsm thickness of galvanising unless the plates are abrasive blasted and more reactive steel is used.[142] There is also the danger that if 600 gsm is achieved that the coating may be brittle. Another consideration is the

---

[141] We used to use nailplates in our bridges painted with micaceous iron oxide. The process involved purchasing the plates, sending them to a galvaniser who pickled them to remove the Z275 coating, hot dipped them and then had them shipped them back. We then had to send them off to a paintshop and then wait for them to be shipped back. There was a long lead time and it was very expensive but also very effective.

[142] McLean, Will. *Pers. Com*. 2 December 2016. Will is Market Development Engineer at the Galvanisers Association of Australia. Specifying the steel will beyond most specifiers.

short design life of Soft Seal of only up to two years.[143] Advice received from the Galvanisers Association of Australia to the author differs slightly from that of Timber Queensland and generally does away with the difference between sheltered and exposed applications. Their recommendation is included as Appendix 1.

The recommendations differ from those of Arch as the Timber Queensland guidelines recognise different risks within the marine environment breaking it up into different risk categories and locations within the building. The Arch guidelines also do not differentiate between a coastal area that has sea spray and a sheltered bayside. But when the extra care needed to make the plate suitable for treated timber is factored in, they are probably little different in practice. Note that in the case of Pryda, the recommendations apply to the whole range of their products, not just nailplates and include post supports. In effect, 316 stainless or equal is recommended for all external applications.

Figure 42.   Test Structure for long term exposure by BRANZ in New Zealand

Finally, consideration has to be given to actual durability trials. The extent of corrosion in fasteners in ACQ and Tanalith E treated timber has generally been assessed by accelerated testing, not through independent inspection of real life or quasi-realistic applications.[144] The conclusion of long term exposure trials conducted by BRANZ concluded in 2011, was that "it was impossible to correlate the corrosion of metal in timber exposed to a high temperature and humidity environment to the corrosion rate under real service conditions".[145] The study went on to conclude that incorrect interpretation of the different accelerated tests has led to incorrect material selection and structural design.[146]

---

[143] CRC Industries (Aust) Pty. Limited. *Technical Data Sheet Product No. 3013,3014, 3015,3016*. URL: http://www.crcindustries.com.au/assets/files/tds/softseal-3013-tds.pdf. Date accessed: 15 December 2016.
[144] Li. *Corrosion ...*, 6.
[145] Li. *Corrosion ...*, 5. These trials were conducted at two sites, one very close to breaking surf and the other five km from a sheltered tidal estuary and protected by hills. These are both areas where manufacturers recommend stainless fasteners but galvanised are frequently used.
[146] Li. *Corrosion...*, 5.

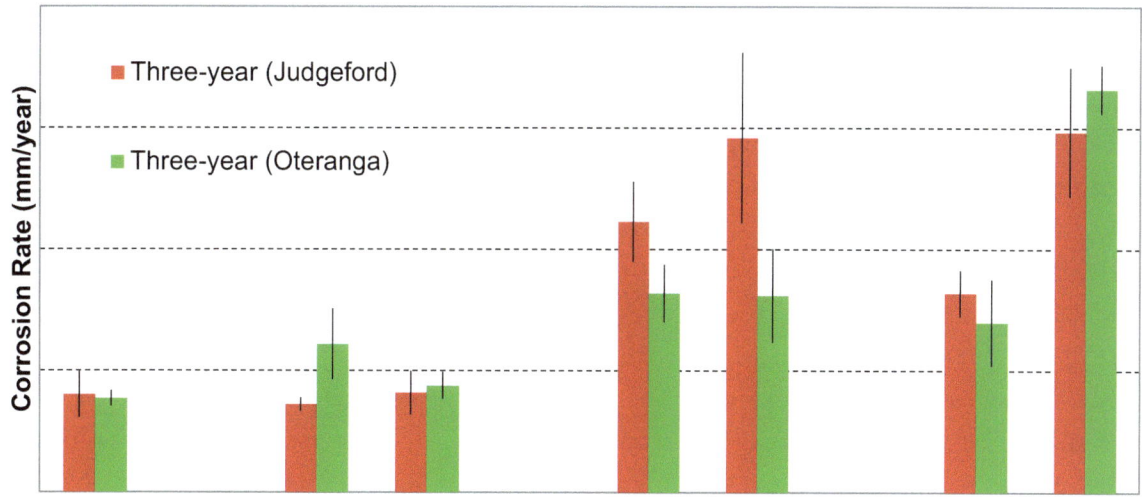

Figure 43. Corrosion rates of hot dipped galvanised nails after three years of exposure in New Zealand. The orange bar is at Oteranga Bay (sea-spray zone) and the red bar is 5 km from a sheltered tidal estuary with hills in-between at Judgeford.

While the chemicals present in the CCA formula are thought to provide passivation effects to the steel, the new chemicals do not contain such inhibitors.[147] Long term testing was undertaken by BRANZ in a relatively benign sheltered marine application, (5 km from an estuary) and in a sea spray zone. The results showed increased early corrosion rates in H4 ACQ of 3.5 times that of H4 CCA in mild steel and at least 7.4 times with fasteners with zinc coatings. That corrosion slowed in time but, after 3 years, the figures were 1.4-1.9 times for mild steel and 3.1-3.6 for zinc. While corrosion of the heads was more in the fasteners closest to the sea, embedded corrosion at the site close to breaking surf was only a little higher and in some cases the shafts had more corrosion in the sheltered area. Among their findings were that:

- mechanically plated screws did not work with any preservative containing copper[148]
- The corrosion behaviour of zinc coated fasteners should be of great concern as, "if the timber gets wet, it is doubtful that hot dip galvanised nails and mechanically-plated screws will be able to meet the durability requirements of the NZBC and relevant New Zealand Codes"[149]
- The sound condition of the head did not necessarily reflect the condition of the shaft[150]
- Stainless performed well without obvious signs of corrosion.[151] Either 316 or 304 should be used as a "sensible interim precaution"[152] to reach the 50-year durability requirement

---

[147] Li. *Corrosion...*, 1.
[148] Li. *Corrosion...*, 65.
[149] Li. *Corrosion...*, 66.
[150] Li. *Corrosion...*, ii.
[151] Li. *Corrosion...*, 65.
[152] Li. *Corrosion...*, 66.

- A lot more work has to be done on researching fasteners under different environments to find out what the long term (>15 years) effects of corrosion are.[153]

The trials also showed that, generally speaking, corrosion severity is as follows: Untreated - CCA - Tanalith E - ACQ[154] which is in same order from low to high of the copper present in the timber. As ACQ and Tanalith E are difficult if not impossible to tell apart and usually specified side by side it is necessary to assume the worst case for corrosion.

Finally, there is one other factor to consider and that is the ductility of the fastener, particularly hardened screws, a factor unrelated to corrosion issues listed above. When these screws are used to fasten timber to steel these screws are prone to snapping and for this reason the major Australian manufacturers will not certify their screws in this application. The hardening process causes the screw to lose its ductility but timber movement, particularly with hardwood, requires that the fastener be ductile. Nails are ductile but the timber movement causes them to come out in decking applications. Conversely, the screw will not come out but, because of its loss of ductility, can snap. One manufacturer reported that this is more of a problem in areas "more than 100 km from the coast as we see greater variance of moisture content with rain and then extremes of dry."[155] Stainless is now all but universally recommended by manufacturers for use as decking screws into steel.

To bring this matter to a conclusion I will quote a considered opinion of one of my newsletter readers; "it is my firm belief that galvanised fasteners are only suitable for timber constructions if the conditions are and continue to be ideal. Due the unpredictability and number of variables that influence exposure conditions as well as the substrate, selecting more corrosion resistant fasteners significantly reduces the risk of premature corrosion."[156]

Alternatives to Stainless Steel Bolts

---

[153] Li. *Corrosion...*, 66.
[154] Kear. *Corrosion...*, 11.
[155] Kuhn, Herb. *Pers. Com.* September 13, 2016. Herb is Managing Director, Simpson Strong-tie Australia.
[156] Duyvestyn, Oscar. *Pers. Com.* June 30, 2016. Oscar is Principal Consultant – Coatings & Advanced Materials with AECOM.

Is there an alternative to stainless steel? Quite possibly, and that is ITW Proline's Tech-Shield™ coated bolts. ITW is the only Australian organisation I am aware of (at the time of writing) which has taken the issue of poor performance of imported galvanised bolts very seriously. At the time of writing this is the only such product on the market in Australia. These bolts have an epoxy coating applied with an electric charge which ensures an even coating. In conjunction with ITW technical coating specialists in Asia and the United States, they developed a new advanced barrier coating that helps bolts protect from the chemicals found in treated timber. This ultimately extends the life of the bolt. When tested at an Independent laboratory to international and Australian standards Tech-Shield™ provided, on average, 3.9 times the protection of their regular hot dipped galvanised bolts when used in treated pine. Unfortunately, they were not available when I operated my business, so I don't have personal experience. Specifiers should check with the manufacturer to determine the suitability of this product for their application.

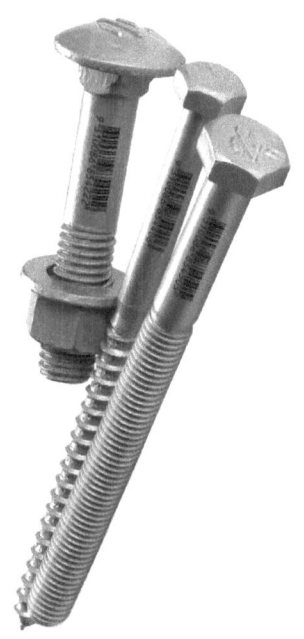

Figure 44. Bolts with corrosion resistant paint.

7 PRESERVATION AND COLOUR

Colour of Preserved Timber

Figure 45. CCA (green) and Tanalith E (natural aged) treated girders.

Figure 46. Treatment Colour Code by AS1604 indicating different treatment levels.

There was a time when many considered that a piece of timber was not properly treated unless it was green, the colour of CCA treatment. But timber treatments now vary dramatically in colour, not only at the point of sale but also as the timber ages. This is partly from the preservatives used and partly from colouring agents added to the treatments. The table below gives some guidance to the colour. Note that not every preservative is suitable for both pine and hardwood and for sawn or natural rounds. An example is natural pine rounds treated to H6. While the timber treats well, the knot cluster does not treat at all and allows for severe degrade and failure of the post.

Treatment Colours			
Chemical	Form	Hardwood	Pine
ACQ	Sawn	Brown and eventually turning natural silver grey	Green turning brown in time
	Round	Brown but quickly turning natural silver grey	Green turning brown in time
Bifenthrin	Sawn	Not normally used	Clear but frequently intentionally tinted
Boron	Sawn	Clear and remaining clear	Clear and remaining clear
	Round	Not normally suitable	Not normally suitable
CCA	Sawn	Green and remaining green	Green and remaining green to brown
	Round	Green and remaining green	Green and remaining green to brown
Creosote	Sawn	Dark brown (rarely used)	Not used
	Rounds	Dark brown (rarely used)	Dark brown
LOSP[201]	Sawn	Natural (seasoned only)	Clear but frequently intentionally tinted
PEC	Sawn	Not used	Not used
	Round	White/brown	White/brown - seldom used
Permethrin	Sawn	Clear when untinted	Clear but frequently tinted
Tanalith E	Sawn	Brown and eventually turning natural silver grey	Green turning brown in time
	Round	Brown but quickly turning natural silver grey	Green turning brown in time
Double treated Marine H6	Sawn	Not suitable	Not suitable
	Round	Dark brown	Not suitable
Table 11.	Treatment colours.		

Additive colourings used on pine framing vary according to its intended use. An example of this can be seen in the products produced by one Queensland manufacturer, Hyne. This company manufactures a range of three treated and coloured pine framing products. The situation in 2020 is as follows: One of the three framings is sold as T2 Blue[tm202] (H2F treatment) which uses an envelope treatment approved in AS1604.1. Being envelope treated the pine is only suitable for use south of the Tropic of Capricorn.[203] Another Hyne product, T2 Red[tm] (a H2 treatment to AS1604.1), has full sapwood penetration. As their framing is made from slash pine where the heartwood is termite resistant[204] there is no need to limit heartwood content in framing as would be necessary with radiata.[205] This more robust treatment makes the timber suitable for use north of the Tropic of Capricorn. The difference is the necessity to deal with

---

[201] Excludes copper naphthenate based LOSP which is green.
[202] T2 Blue, T2 red and T3 Green are registered trademarks of Hyne.
[203] http://www.hyne.com.au/our_business/hyne_t2blue.html Accessed May 15, 2011.
[204] AS 5604 – 2005 Table A1. Note it is "termite resistant" not "termite proof".
[205] Radiata can still meet the H2 requirements by either carefully selecting the timber for sapwood content or by incising.

Mastotermes darwinensis (giant northern termites).[206] Hyne's third coloured framing, T3 Green[tm] (H3 to AS 1604.1)[207] is azole permethrin treated, an LOSP treatment.[208] All these products come with a 25-year guarantee. The envelope treatment of T2 Blue means that there is a very small uptake of chemical so duplicated stock holding is economical. Treatment processes and chemicals are available from a range of suppliers, and while manufactures are free to change processes, chemical suppliers and chemicals for economic reasons the treatment colour coding remains fixed. In the framing market there is a variety of trade names and processes, but they all use the same colour coding system as stipulated in AS 1604.1 – 2012.[209] The hues vary between chemical suppliers, however. With the possibility of colour changes within an order, if the colour is important it is necessary to plan for this by specifying that a uniform hue is achieved.

These colours are achieved by proprietary methods which utilise either dyes or pigments and are required under AS 1604.1 – 2012 to be light-fast[210]. They should retain their colour in visible weather-protected applications. However, while red and green colour coding may be acceptable to some in visible timber, blue invariably is not. In reality, the red and green are not an architectural quality finish, and most would think it needs enhancing if the timber is going to be visible. The colourfastness is said to vary dramatically depending on the colourants used by the preservative manufacturer. If colour coded timber is an issue e.g. in architectural trusses or a shelter shed, The end user should seek out a custom treater who offers clear treatment.

Pigmented treatments for weather exposed pine have been available in the UK and in the USA for some years for waterborne preservatives such as Tanalith E. The tinted treatment for that system in the UK is called Tanatone[tm211]. This additive enables the pine to achieve a permanent rich brown colour, as opposed to its normal green (turning a light brown) when Tanalith E treated. Because the brown colouring is primarily aesthetic, it needs more care. The manufacturer recommends:

> "Timber which is rip sawn, equalised, planed or heavily sanded must be returned to the treatment plant for re-treatment. On no account are fence posts to be pointed after treatment. The shortening of posts and columns should be avoided. In any event cross cutting must be restricted to the top of the post or column".[212]

Products such as Tanatone[tm] are now becoming available on the Australian market and can be expected to represent a significant section of the treatment market. Australian trials have found that there is sufficient colourfastness for the Australian climate, which was an issue with early colourants.[213]

---

[206] http://www.hyne.com.au/t2red/index.html Accessed May 15, 2011.
[207] http://www.hyne.com.au/our_business/hyne_t3green.html Accessed May 15, 2011.
[208] Stringer, Geoff. *Pers. Com.* May 16, 2011.
[209] Clause 1.7.7 Table 3.
[210] AS 1604.1 – 2010 requires a colour fastness rating of 7 to ISO 12040 which in clause 4.2.2 is rated as "excellent" but industry contacts indicate that this is not always achieved and is probably not necessary. The framing only needs to be sufficiently colourfast for the three to four months of the building project.
[211] Tanatone is a registered trademark of Arch Timber Protection.
[212] Arch Chemicals. http://resources.pihomebuild.com/sites/478/docs/specifiers_guide_tan_e.pdf.
[213] Koch, Steve. Australian Customer Service Manager, Arch Wood Protection (Aust) Pty Limited. *Pers. Com.* May 16, 2011.

Colour as an Indication of Successful Treatment

When looking at a piece of treated structural hardwood, where the colour of the treatment is not modified by stains, but just that of the treatment itself, a purchaser expects to see a strong uniform colour. Is its absence an indication of inadequate treatment? There are two main visual indicators that give rise to concern - blotchy treatment and a lighter colour than expected.

"Blotchy" Treatment

Figure 47. Apparent non treatment of timber.

Figure 48. Full sapwood penetration was still achieved.

Occasionally I, or more correctly my customers, have observed and complained about what can best be called "blotchy" treatment where the surface colouring from the treatment chemical is not uniform. It gives the impression that the timber has not been treated correctly. When taking a sample of the timber (shown above) and checking the penetration of the sapwood, full penetration was achieved i.e. treatment was achieved despite appearances. This surface "blotchiness" is caused by treating timber that has been rained on and has moisture on the surfaces inside the pack. It is only cosmetic. The hardwood treater makes no other claims than that the sapwood is fully penetrated with preservative at the correct level.

Light uniform colour is sometimes an indicator of low treatment but is no more than that. The image shows CCA treated eucalypt timber in a lodge I stayed in while visiting Tanzania.[214] The green tinge is barely visible. I probed the support posts under the deck which were a darker green (because they are out of the sun) but were still very light. They were showing severe decay after only five years.

Figure 49. Light coloured CCA treatment in Tanzania.

---

[214] Arch's African guarantee for 50 years for H3 and 25 years for H5 only covers timber treated in South Africa and Swaziland. This is probably wise. The guarantee was found at http://www.archchemicals.com/Fed/WOODSA/Docs/Guarantee_Brochure.pdf.

Unfortunately, timber that is correctly treated has a wide range of shades and can have a lighter colour than expected. Colour itself cannot be relied upon as an indicator of effective treatment.[215]

---

[215] The second deck in five years was just about ready to be replaced. When I spoke with the management there was no comprehension about how to do a deck well and no willingness to spend the extra to do it well despite such short service lives.

8 WHEN IS A PRESERVATIVE NOT A PRESERVATIVE

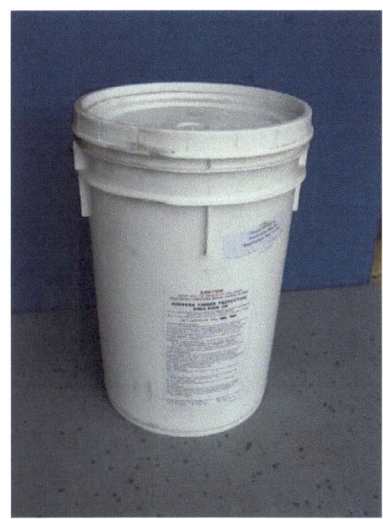 

Figure 50. CN Emulsion and CN Oil are examples of useful but non-permanent preservatives.

To design professionals, the word "preservative" should conjure up well proven timber preservatives such as CCA, Tanalith E and ACQ. They would also be very aware of the different hazard levels from H1 through to H6. These preservatives are impregnated into the timber through a variety of processes using very expensive machinery under controlled and monitored conditions. Timber treated to these levels does not come with an expiry date! What then does the word "preservative" on a can of a "paint-on" product imply?

The term "preservative" is controlled by the APVMA, so a manufacturer cannot legally call a product a "preservative" unless the APVMA has been provided with, and has accepted, scientific evidence that the product is effective in a certain application and make very specific claims about the duration of its effectiveness. An example is Thomson White's In-Ground Paste, a copper napthenate (CN) emulsion paste. On the can we read where the product is to be used – "Situation: Timber already in use or treated according to AS1604 and in ground contact or other damp situations. We also read its "effectiveness". Retreatment should be done every 3 to 5 years. So clearly, this in-ground "preservative" does not have the effectiveness that you are expecting from H rated preservatives. It is really only a supplemental aid – not the prime treatment of the timber.

There is still a valuable place for such products, and we would not consider building a structure without treating cut ends and timber-to-timber interfaces with a CN Emulsion. But such products must not be considered as a substitute for correct preservative treatment and correct selection of natural durability. CCA has good UV blocking ability (not ACQ or Tanalith E) whereas neither CCA, ACQ nor Tanalith E are water repellents. Their effectiveness is enhanced by products such as OSA's Tanacoat which contain both water repellents and UV blockers.

When considering the use of paint-on "preservatives" read the claims very carefully. Does it have any? I was not able to find any paint-on product that will achieve H3 or better protection. During 2007, OSA was instrumental in reporting a decking oil manufacturer to the APVMA, and action was taken because of making unsubstantiated preservative claims about its product.

A note on the use of CN Emulsion: Degrade at the end grain due to moisture absorption is an area of design that has to be addressed seriously. CN emulsion is effective in countering this. The label directs that a 6mm coating be applied and it readily absorbs into the end grain. On naturally durable and already treated hardwood timber-to-timber interfaces where enhanced durability and water repellence is required, the application of CN Emulsion is also recommended. If the emulsion is applied 6mm thick (in accordance with the manufacturer's instructions) it will simply squeeze out and contaminate the surroundings. We recommend no more than a 1mm, maximum 2mm coating in these applications.

Metal Based Preservatives are not Insect Repellents

Figure 51. Cylindrical Auger Beetle attack.   Figure 52. Cylindrical Auger Beetle..

Over the thirty years that I have been producing timber products, there have been a few (and only a few) occasions when insect attack on freshly sawn timber has been brought to my attention. These infestations have always occurred in clusters with considerable periods between reports. The last outbreak was in 2007 and at the time, Lonza, the supplier of our treatment chemical, advised that others had experienced the same attack.

With each infestation the same beetle was involved, the cylindrical auger beetle. Fortunately, the infestation is only short lived as the insects desist after the timber has dried and cause no structural damage. F14, a common specification but a very low grade for most unseasoned Queensland hardwood[216] has no limit to the number of these pinholes and F17 allows 20 holes in a 100x100 section. That is not to discount the aesthetics of course.

Metal based timber treatment only affects the sapwood and does not work as an insect repellent. Any insect that burrows, without actually eating the timber is not affected by the treatment. Should eggs be laid, and they hatch out, the larvae are killed once they eat treated timber. This breaks the life cycle. When the timber dries there is no further attack. However, permethrin and bifenthrin, common active ingredients in LOSP and glueline preservatives, are repellants.

---

[216] E.g., spotted gum, ironbark and blackbutt, an exception is forest red gum.

9 SPECIAL CONSIDERATIONS WITH CCA

How Dangerous is CCA?

While the western world has largely turned its back on CCA, worldwide it is still the most common preservative.[217] Is the widespread use of CCA then just a matter of poverty taking the less expensive option without due regard to the health of users? Or is it a reasonable response to the evidence?

When the APVMA reviewed the scientific studies into CCA, which probably range into the multi thousand, it concluded:

> "Based on a consideration of the exposure to CCA treated timber products, in particular children's play equipment, there was no compelling evidence from the available data to conclude that there was likely to be an unacceptable risk to public health from arsenic from CCA treated timber."[218]

Their conclusion, in face of this less than overwhelming evidence, was "Evidence of health problems associated with this use has not been proven. Because arsenic at higher levels is a carcinogen, and alternative wood preservatives are available, restrictions in some domestic applications will occur as a precaution."[219]

CCA was removed from segments of the Australian market, not because it was proven dangerous but because it was not proven safe. Unfortunately, the APVMA could not agree with the industry on the format of test regime whereby it may be proven to be safe.

The New Zealand Authorities reviewed the same data and came to a different conclusion. Their report said "CCA-treated wood has also been in use for many years without discernible health effects suggesting that if there is a true increased risk it is very small".[220] The New Zealanders attempted to quantify the risk in that country. They maintain that an increased risk of one in 100,000 over a 70 year lifetime from exposure to a carcinogen was acceptable.[221] The actual risk is far less than this.[222] Bear in mind that the very visit to a playground is probably more dangerous. There are said to be in the order of 250,000 playground injuries in Australia each year, these are real injuries and should put the unproven risk of CCA into perspective![223]

---

[217] Jensen. Greg. *Pers. Com.* Feb 12, 2012.
[218] APVMA. The Reconsideration of Registrations of Arsenic Timber Treatment Products (CCA and arsenic trioxide) and Their Associated Labels - Report Of Review Findings And Regulatory Outcomes Final Report Part 1 - Toxicological Assessment (Canberra, 2005) 19. The APVMA report was found at http://www.apvma.gov.au/products/review/docs/arsenic_tox.pdf.
[219] CSIRO. *The Facts about CCA treated timber Page 7.* http://www.csiro.au/en/Outcomes/Food-and-Agriculture/CCATreatedTimber/CCA-safety-overview.aspx Date accessed, 21 April 2012.
[220] Read, Deborah. *Report on Copper Chrome and Arsenic Treated Timber.* ERMANZ April 2003 http://archive.ermanz.govt.nz/resources/publications/pdfs/cca-report.pdf. Date accessed, 21 April 2012, 57.
[221] Read. *Report...,* 57.
[222] Read. *Report...,* 56-9.
[223] This figure was mentioned at a Kidsafe conference I spoke at a few years ago. Kidsafe Victoria give actual hospitalisations from playground injuries at 6000 per year or roughly 10% of all children's admissions. Kidsafe Victoria, *Action to Reduce Playground Injuries,* http://www.kidsafevic.com.au/news/25-action-to-reduce-playground-injuries. Date accessed 28 May

The New Zealand study makes the observation "Despite uncertainty and potential overestimation of cancer risk it would be prudent public health policy to reduce human exposure to arsenic from all sources wherever feasible".[224] Yet the implications of this statement are enormous. When we tested our employees for arsenic levels it was essential that they did not drink beer or eat seafood for three days beforehand. If they did eat or drink these common items they could give a false high reading because of their arsenic content. Wouldn't consistency also require that these also be banned?

But facts are worth very little when dealing with grandmothers who grew up with *Arsenic and Old Lace* and young mothers who saw the fictional account of CCA poisoning in *The Practice*. There are alternatives available to counter these perceptions and it is simply much easier to use them than to fight against the tide. While there are alternatives to CCA available for most applications, it is not simply a matter of specifying Tanalith E treated to H5 instead of CCA treated to H5 (which in many cases was over-specification). Because of the much higher chemical cost and the availability of plants licensed to treat to the higher levels, these alternative treatments will probably not be realisable. As mentioned earlier, they simply never were achievable in sawn timber.

Take care when specifying "timber treatments" to ensure you do not put yourself in a situation that may require future remedial action or client complaints. CCA is still legal for some products such as commercial decking (but illegal for domestic) but may still be rejected by the client.[225]

Figure 53. A cartoon on the dangers of CCA.

A few years ago, I spoke at a timber treaters' conference and while there spoke with a representative of the APVMA. I asked, "Have all the products that are used in children's playgrounds been subject to the same scrutiny as CCA." The reply was "I hope so." The fact is they have not been. This was confirmed 12 months later when I spoke at a Kidsafe conference on the subject of treating. During lunch I sat near two manufacturers of rubber soft fall and they were expressing concern about the safety of their product. I have not been able to find studies on rubber soft fall but like CCA it should be thoroughly

---

2012. Estimates of the number of injuries vary greatly. I have seen figures quoted varying between 100,000 to 500,000!
[224] Read. *Report...*, 62.
[225] A guide to acceptable use is available at http://www.outdoorstructures.com.au/pdf/cca_acceptable_usage.pdf. Not every application is covered in this list, e.g. bollards.

investigated.[226] The likely scenario is that when all the products that we use in children's playground have been subject to the same scrutiny as CCA there is likely to be nothing left to design with!

CCA Fixation

Unlike other preservatives, CCA must undergo a period of "fixation" which stops the migration of the chemicals. The copper and arsenic components of CCA work as fungicides and insecticides. Chrome is added to fix these chemicals to the timber. This fixation does not happen until a chemical reaction occurs within the timber. This reaction sees the "reduction of chromium from the hexavalent to the trivalent state, and the subsequent precipitation or adsorption of chromium, copper and arsenic complexes in the wood substrate."[227]

When we were manufacturing CCA treated powerpoles we had to hold the poles in stock for six weeks after treatment to ensure fixation. When I enquired about the reasoning behind this, mention was made of a Canadian study which showed that, in mid-winter, with presumably two feet of snow on top, it did take this time. Fortunately, we treated in sunny Queensland where the weather is "beautiful one day and perfect the next". Fortunately, also, it has long been known that the time taken to fix CCA is temperature related. One study showed that adequate fixation could be achieved in only 120 hours at 25 C (77 F).[228] In midsummer at 30 C (or even much higher), holding timber to ensure fixation becomes a meaningless concept. Despite this, we were contractually bound to hold pole stock for six weeks which caused untold and unnecessary complications and additional cost which was passed on. Steam conditioning is a process that can be used to further reduce this time also but seems pointless in the warmer states.

When I proposed relaxing this extended period and introducing a simple and established chemical test to establish fixation, this was not accepted by our customer. It appeared that it was a case of regulation for the sake of regulation. As for material that was not contracted we did not hold material once it was dry as we figured the remaining part of the short process could take place just as easily out in the open on site as it would out in the open in our yard. No-one held six weeks treatment under roof.

What can be Done with Existing CCA Infrastructure?

Figure 54.   Leaching Trials.

Figure 55.   Contact Trials.

[226] Smith, A.H. Duggan, H.M. Wright C *Assessment of cancer clusters using limited cohort data with spreadsheets: application to a leukaemia cluster among rubber workers* American Journal of Industrial Medicine, 1994 Jun;25(6):813-23 may be relevant.
[227] Lebow, Stan. *Fixation of CCA*. (Granbury: American Wood Preservers' Association. 1998) 1.
[228] Leblow. *Fixation...,* 1

If asset owners are not prepared to maintain their structures, they should pull them out immediately, whether they are made of steel or timber, untreated or treated. Surely the danger from a loose bolt is more real (and likely) than a possible risk from treatment? Wise asset management dictates that timber infrastructure should be regularly maintained with a simple, effective maintenance program, regardless of the treatment employed. This maintenance program should include the simplest preparation and re-application techniques. Preparation should be able to be performed quickly by unskilled labour. The product best fitting this description is penetrating oil.

The APVMA has no regulatory authority over existing structures constructed of CCA treated timber and so has made no recommendation with respect to future action for existing structures. To date, regulatory authorities in the USA, Europe and Canada have not recommended dismantling existing structures. However, the APVMA is aware that the USEPA is conducting an extensive assessment of this issue.

CCA treated timber which is processed in Australia is now illegal for many traditional applications. Serious concern (and almost panic) has been expressed in many quarters about what to do with existing CCA structures. Understandably asset owners simply did not know what to do with existing CCA treated infrastructure, while the APVMA did not require existing CCA timber to be removed even from children's playgrounds and their ruling gave no clear guidance as to what to do with it. Sealing the timber with a penetrating oil was suggested as a potential effective solution. They said:

> "Information is limited on the possible benefits of painting treated-timber (including existing structures) to reduce possible risks. Some scientific studies indicate that certain penetrating coatings, such as oil-based semi-transparent stains, when used on a regular basis **_may_**[229] reduce the potential for CCA exposure. However, there have been some questions raised about the effectiveness of film-forming or non-penetrating stains because of cracking, peeling and flaking".[230]

This suggestion is exactly the same as wise asset management. However, the APVMA says MAY reduce exposure. Does it in actual fact work?

OSA asked Arch Chemicals who manufacture Tanacoat for us to undertake testing to determine if this sealing does in fact happen. Tanacoat has been proven to be remarkably effective in sealing CCA treated timber. Under laboratory simulation, leaching of the active constituents was reduced by 50% and transfer by physical contact to virtually one twentieth.[231] So, applying Tanacoat to timber allows the asset owner to maintain good timber maintenance practices and deal with CCA at the same time.[232]

CCA Treatment and Fire
A long time ago we installed new cattle fencing in some timber land we owned at the time. We used split hardwood posts which are normal posts used in that location. As the posts contained sapwood,

---

[229] Underlining and bold added by author.
[230] APVMA, *Reconsideration ...*, 15.
[231] Detailed results are found at
http://www.outdoorstructures.com.au/pdf/cca_timber_treatment_analysis.pdf
and the methodology used is found at
http://www.outdoorstructures.com.au/pdf/cca_timber_treatment_methodology.pdf.
[232] Further information on sealing CCA can be found on the USEPA website:
http://www.epa.gov/scipoly/sap/meetings/2006/november/november2006finalmeetingminutes.pdf.

which was going to decay, I thought I would be wise and treat the posts with CCA. The logic was hard to fault at the time, but the end result was the opposite of what we intended. When the first fire came through, normally not much of an issue, we lost most of the posts which burned completely to the ground. I learnt very quickly that there can be a major issue with CCA treatment and fire.

Figure 56. Fire has destroyed a new boardwalk.

My fence was nobody's fault but mine and was completely unintentional. You can only wonder at the mentality of people who intentionally destroy infrastructure, built for their enjoyment and the enjoyment of others. As much as we cannot understand it, vandalism by fire is a reality has to be considered. 0 shows graphically how a treated structure can succumb to fire. Increased resistance to fire can be achieved by using timbers with a low spread of flame index, applying an intumescent paint or by using fire retardant treatments.

Increasing fire Resistance of treated timber

Intumescent Paint
Normally a grass fire burns rapidly, and, with relatively short grass, it passes under the boardwalk doing little if any damage. This was obviously not the case shown in 0. This boardwalk, built approximately 2001, was situated in a swamp and went through long grass. In the middle of a drought, when it was only days old, someone set the grass alight. The fire was intense, and the long burning grass fell across the full length of the boardwalk and the whole structure burnt to the ground. Our first thought was that the CN oil that we had used to coat the bearers, joists and decking was the reason for losing the structure so completely. But when we checked with the manufacturer, we learnt that the flashpoint of the oil was very similar to that of the hardwood used and so there was no increased fire risk with oiling. The problem was simply that there was a source of flame over the whole length of boardwalk instead of a localized flame that you get with normal vandalism. This poor boardwalk did not stand a chance.

The intense fire also saw the unoiled CCA H5 pine posts burn to the ground. It is difficult to find a better foundation than a H5 CCA pine post. It has a design life of 50 years, is light and inexpensive. They are also easy to carry to sites with poor access. The drawback is that when they are subject to fire they can experience "afterglow", a phenomenon whereby when after the fire source is removed, they continue burning because of the effect of the preservatives. The replacement boardwalk was re-built in timber, but this time consideration was given to how to avoid a repeat performance.

The posts, bearers, joists and the underside and sides of the decking were painted with Luxury Paints fire retardant paint. The paint was tinted to be less obvious. The paint system was not considered robust enough to be used on the face of the decking. The rebuilt boardwalk was still performing well at the time of writing. How big a problem is fire in a hardwood boardwalk? To my knowledge this is the only one I have lost in 14 years. We occasionally are called for a few replacement boards but that is all. By careful choice of species with low Early Fire Index you can reduce the risk to an acceptable level. Remember the ubiquitous F14, F17 specification does not address this, but our Deckwood and Joistwood specification does. We deal with fire in our Boardwalk Design Guide.

Figure 57. CCA pine post with intumescent paint used in conjunction with fire resistant hardwood

Pine of course is a different matter. It has an affinity with fire regardless of the treatment.

Treatment and Fire-Retardants
Just as treating my fence posts with CCA was a reasonable assumption, so is adding an impregnated (as opposed to a paint-on) fire retardant to try and ensure the integrity of a structure during fire. Unfortunately, because of the presence of phosphorus, some fire retardants can counteract the effect of the treatment and lead to premature failure. This can probably be countered by adding even more preservative it was reported[233] however there were no data available to determine what these levels should be. A specifier should be careful when trying to combine the treatment with fire retardants and should seek written advice from both the preservative and the fire-retardant suppliers.[234]

---

[233] Jensen, Greg. *Pers. Com.* 9 January 2012.
[234] I encountered such a specification for a large boardwalk in Singapore. Despite supplying a letter from the manufacturer of both the preservative and the fire retardant that they were not compatible and a shorter life would result, the specification was not modified!

10 PRESERVATION WARRANTIES

Changing Nature of Warranties

Timber treated to the now repealed Acts or the Australian Standard does not come with a nominated service life. Behind a wall and in the absence of fire there is no reason why, with some treatments, you cannot talk about a possible life span in the hundreds of years. This is not the case when the timber is exposed to the weather or used in ground. To add confidence and as a marketing aid, manufacturers of treatment chemicals, or the manufacturer themselves, may give a warranty on timber treated with their products. The existence of warranties from a chemical supplier is surprising. A chemical supplier was warranting a product made by someone else that they did not have full control over. The early warranties said nothing meaningful so there was little risk, but the warranties developed from simple replacement to reinstatement,[235] so the situation is now remarkable.

A review of the guarantees available before the Introduction of the Australian Consumer Law in January 2011 showed that they only covered insect, borer and fungal attack. Typically, they initially only covered the original purchaser for the replacement of the timber without the associated rectification costs or associated losses. Degrade such as the physical destruction of the pine decking through constant wetting and drying was not covered. As well, the warranties did not extend to commercial projects. An example of an older style warranty is the Koppers Hickson "lifetime" guarantee which extended from the time the person purchased the timber to however long they owned the property.[236] Rights of redress under this warranty for Queensland and New South Wales residents would have been far less than if they had taken action under their State's timber protection laws. As warranties evolved to the point where reinstatement also was covered, the difficulty remained of putting years to a life expectancy when the Standards and timber protection Acts did not. The Building Code of Australia mentions a design life of 50 years which led to public expectancy that guarantees should match but some guarantees are for only half this period.

The 2011 Act did away with the expression "merchantable quality" and replaced it with, "acceptable quality" which in its definition contains an express element of 'durability'. "If a product is not sufficiently durable (such that it breaks down earlier than a consumer would reasonably expect) then it is no longer necessary to prove that it had a latent defect at the time of supply – all a consumer needs to establish is that a product failed early and was therefore not sufficiently durable".[237] There are now nine consumer guarantees in the Act which clarify rather than extend consumer rights. The Act introduces the idea of major failure where the customer determines the remedy and a minor failure where the supplier decides. Without manufacturer's warranties, the purchaser now has very strong rights for redress.

Manufacturer's warranties must not only protect the consumer guarantees mandated in the Act but also draw attention to them through the words *"Our goods come with guarantees that cannot be excluded under the Australian Consumer Law. You are entitled to a replacement or refund for a major failure and for compensation for any other reasonably foreseeable loss or damage. You are also entitled to have the goods repaired or replaced if the goods fail to be of acceptable quality and the failure does not amount*

---

[235] Koppers Performance Chemicals. *Wood Product Warranty 2016.* 2.

[236] This guarantee was still on the Dindas website at the time of writing despite the changeover to Koppers Arch and then Arch many years ago. The address was http://dindas.com.au/pdf/warranty.pdf.

[237] Ebsworth H.W.L. *Australian Consumer Law – Summary of changes.* January 2011 URL http://www.hwlebsworth.com.au/files/TP.pdf. Date Accessed 12 January 2012.

to a major failure."

Warranties were rewritten to reflect the new Act. As an example, the new warranty issued by Arch included a warranty period with different responses depending on age, in the case of H3 General Use this covered product and labour costs for up to 10 years' service, and then up to 25 years just material replacement. H3 Decking is 7 and 15 years respectively. It is difficult to see any likelihood of a claim.

One manufacturer reported[238] that there are very few complaints about performance that proceed to actual warranty claims. Poor building practice, described as something outside of the Building Code, will negate a claim, and reasonably so, as is using timber outside of the H level it was treated to. Most claims are for H3 treated product, e.g. H3 pine decking that someone has set pot plants on (raising this to H4 actual) or use of H3 pine in a tropical rainforest (really a H4 application despite being officially classed as H3). In the drafting of the revised warranty it is understood that the intent was initially only to cover treated fibres and not untreated/untreatable timber. This has been an emphasis of this book. The wording was changed to cover the whole piece with treated and untreated fibres so long as it was treated and used in accordance with recognized standards.[239] The warranty was extended to cover commercial, but not public infrastructure.

There has since been a further change in direction with warranties with some manufactures withdrawing their blanket consumer warranty entirely. In light of the long list of exclusions highlighting bad practice that would be necessary, and the strength of the new consumer legislation, a warranty that a treatment chemical manufacturer may offer a consumer becomes somewhat pointless. This has been replaced with a commitment to support the treater in the event of a problem; something I have found had always been present. At the time of reviewing this guide in 2015, the industry is again in transition with some treaters having a chemical manufacturers warranty that extends to their consumers and others not. It is anticipated that all consumer warranties from the treatment chemical manufacturers will be phased out over time. We are increasingly seeing timber manufacturers providing their own warranties now. The two examples below show how a warranty may or may not apply.

Warranty Example 1

Figure 58. Degrade of pine decking after nine years.

The image in 0 shows a piece of very weathered treated pine at a large holiday complex at Caloundra that was only nine years old. The whole deck needed to be replaced. Earlier treatment chemical manufacturer's warranties excluded commercial applications from claims but even with the increased scope of cover of later warranties there is no valid claim against a treatment manufacturer's warranty in this instance - the timber has neither decayed nor has it been attacked by insects. The decking is self-destructing as the species choice was poor. A durable hardwood such as spotted gum or Ironbark should have been specified. A timber manufacturer may choose to warrant the treated timber he produces for this application, but it would seem imprudent to do so other than a normal defects warranty of twelve years.

---

[238] Jensen, Greg. *Pers. Com.* 12 January 2012.
[239] Arch Wood Protection (Aust) Pty Ltd. *Tanalised Outdoor Wood Guarantee*: January 2012.

Warranty Example 2[240]

Figure 59. "Treated" timber that has decayed in concrete

Should a piece of Blackbutt without sapwood be coloured with CCA, it can be stamped H5 because it is a Durability Class 2 and no penetration is required for H4 and H5. It can be then set in concrete and still follow the Building Code. All of this is poor supply and building practice but meets all necessary codes despite being well recognised as bad practice. A failure within a 25-year period is entirely possible. Where a chemical manufacturer's consumer warranty has been withdrawn there would be no claim against them. However, the timber supplier may choose to provide the consumer with their own warranty.

The situation now is that material already on the market is protected by a variety of warranties and Acts. When purchasing new material, a consumer needs to determine from his supplier prior to purchase what warranty is being offered. If a warranty is available care must then be taken to obtain a copy.

---

[240] I have chosen this example as ground line attack has been demonstrated to be a problem of particular concern in my home locality, the Lockyer Valley. Leightley. *Technical...*, 9, c.f. Greaves. *Inspection...*, 15 .

11 SAMPLING, TESTING AND DUE DILIGENCE

Lack of a National Quality Program

As has been mentioned, there was initially a very effective quality program run by the Queensland and New South Wales state governments that monitored the compliance with the relevant timber marketing Acts in those states. Treaters had to prove initially that they could treat to the requirements of their respective Acts and then, through regular monitoring, prove that they could maintain compliance. While I recall some bumps along the way, the introduction of easy access to independent laboratory testing of samples meant that it was possible to accurately monitor the conformance of any product produced. The situation now is that there is no state or national quality assurance program in place. Such schemes exist in Europe and even South Africa so its absence in Australia is a severe shortcoming in the industry and this is usually put down simply to the industry being unwilling to shoulder the associated costs.

This does not mean that all treatment is poorly done or even most of it. There are very ethical and risk averse suppliers who as part of their quality assurance will:

- Maintain charge sheets that monitor each stage of each batch of treated timber
- Reconcile chemical usage against the volume treated.
- Conduct sampling and analysis that is statistically relevant and
    - Will reduce sampling if good results are maintained.
    - Will Increase sampling if failures occur.

While minimising risk and increasing customer confidence the outcome of this monitoring benefits the producer also by allowing them to minimise overtreatment and so not pay for more chemical more than needed. But without a national scheme in place the possibility exists for someone to import timber that has been treated overseas from countries where these controls may not always exist and even use species that are not easily treated. It is only necessary to claim, not prove compliance to AS1604.1. The risk is that product from a reputable supplier may be substituted by a lower cost product without the necessary verification programs. Verification of compliance to a specified H level should be part of a designer's arsenal as he/she attempts to deliver a successful project.

When should timber be tested?

The standards give no guidance on when timber should be tested. In the absence of a national quality assurance scheme I can only give some guidelines. Generally, the risk with H2S material is low but not non-existent. Failures I have seen have almost always been with H3 applications and up. You should consider testing when:

- Compliance is critical. If the concrete needs to be tested for compliance, then in my opinion the timber does also
- The branding out of place for the application – refer Figure 35
- There is no branding at all – refer Figure 35
- Product substitution has taken place
- Hardwood been requested at H4 and above, (this is labour and time consuming to successfully achieve); and,
- When there is a breakdown in trust

An area where there is little risk and where there would be little value in testing would be applications up to H3 with waterborne preservatives in hardwoods which have high durability. It is very easy to achieve this level of treatment and, as has been discussed, the amount of treatable sapwood present may not cause a structural issue if it did fail.

Sampling Process

There are guidelines to the sampling process in *AS/NZS1605.1-2018 - Methods for sampling and analysing timber preservatives and preservative-treated timber, Part 1: General requirements, sampling, and determination of sapwood and heartwood presence.* But it is not necessary, however, to be familiar with the standard. What is necessary is to contact the specialist laboratory you plan to use prior to any sampling. They will advise you on the type and size of sample taken and the number that will be necessary to make a meaningful report based on their knowledge of the standard and changes that are proposed at the time of writing. Guidelines will be something like:

Sawn and round timber and LVL. – a cross section normally 300 mm long and free of knots and other defects as well as staples and fasteners.
Plywood with glueline treatment. - a section 200x220 mm from anywhere in the piece.
Borings. – a core at least 30 mm in diameter for up to H5 and 40 mm for H6. Larger core samples should be taken if possible.

Figure 60. Sample collection by boring.

Figure 61. Sampling of H4 treated hardwood

The samples need to be clearly identified with whatever specific identification that is required for the report. Ensure the area that the sample is taken from is also clearly marked with matching identification. A second sample should be retained or given to the builder/supplier as, in the event of a failure, they will need to undertake confirmation sampling. (Note that the third sample in 0 was taken for species identification) For transit, borings should be packed in corrugated cardboard and cushioned with bubble wrap. Paperwork that will accompany the samples may be generated from the laboratory's website but will include the site location and what hazard level to test for.

When taking samples from hardwood it is critical that you select a piece that has a significant amount of sapwood. Consider where the best place to sample is. If timber is shipped to site and found to have failed the treatment requirements it can be very expensive to return.

Due Diligence when Selling Treated Timber.

I was once involved in a consultancy that was a nightmare for all concerned. A project in an area with high termite activity was specified in cypress. The owner was very aware of the effective termite resistance of cypress, but the builder substituted treated radiata. This is not an issue if the timber was treated correctly. I was called in to take samples for testing to determine if the timber was treated to code. In areas where there was access to the framing, I found timber from two producers, one failed and one passed. Whose framing was it behind the sheeted walls? This experience taught or reinforced to me:

- The value of not mixing suppliers of framing
- The importance of maintaining records of who produced the framing: and,
- Timber framing must never be purchased on price but always compliance to the specification,

The Frame and Truss Manufacturers Association of Australia give guidance as to the minimum record keeping that should be undertaken by their members. They have recognized that there is going to be increasing requests by builders and certifiers to receive a single compliance certificate (0) from the processor. The Association advises:

> "It is important that fabricators do their due diligence and request their timber suppliers send their relevant warranty/guarantee information for you to file within your business. Create a Timber Treatment File and then create a folder for each timber supplier and store their compliance and warranty documentation on file. Furthermore, it is vital that fabricators fully read and understand the various warranties and manufacturers guidelines and comply with any necessary product requirements."[241]

Further, to keep the supply chain tidy they advise against stocking white pine and sending it for treatment when required but instead to only purchase already treated timber.[242]

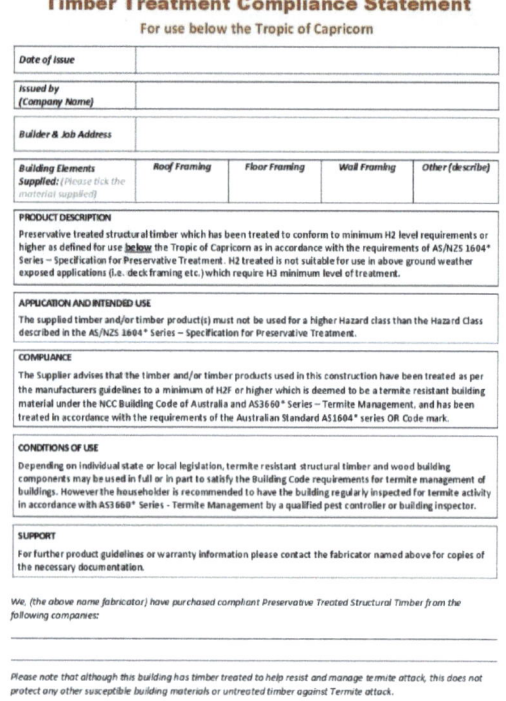

Figure 62.   Sample compliance certificate

---

[241] Frame and Truss Manufacturers Association of Australia. *Timber Treatment Compliance, Fabricators must do Due Diligence.* No publication details.
[242] Frame. *Timber …,*

12 SOME PRESERVATION CASE HISTORIES

Some durability/serviceability issues with timber are very complex and the following real-life case history will assist the reader work through the issues of species properties, natural durability, design and preservation

CityCat Terminals - A Natural Durability/Preservation Dilemma

Figure 63.   Rubbing strips on CityCat terminals.

Figure 64.   Bolts heads are quickly exposed as the timber wears.

The old ferry terminals on the brackish Brisbane River were built on turpentine piles, the only commercially available Australian hardwood with sufficient durability to withstand marine borer attack. With the introduction of the modern CityCat service, modern materials were chosen to build the new terminals. But the problem arose of how to stop the CityCats damaging themselves when moored up against the now steel piles. The answer - old tech timber. The piles have fenders made of profiled timber rubbing strips ex. 100x50 which are mounted in a frame that attaches to the steel pile. These frames can be replaced as a unit when the strips are worn out. Outdoor Structures Australia supplied many of these rubbing strips. Standing out from the terminals are free standing steel piles which the CityCats skew against to make quick changes in direction.

There are two requirements for these strips to succeed
- strong resistance to abrasion and impact
- high resistance to marine borer attack

For the first property the material of choice would be spotted gum. It is naturally greasy so the boats would rub against it without damage to the aluminium hull. Spotted gum is also the material of choice for Australian manufacturers of striking tool handles. It is also a traditional material for all components in boat building but, in that case, it would be used with anti-fouling paint.[243] Turpentine has the required

---

[243] Despite its traditional use for this application, being in the lowest category of marine durability does make its use in ship building questionable and must surely have required considerable maintenance.

amount of resistance to marine borer attack but does not have good impact resistance. OSA supplied the rubbing strips in both species and neither was very satisfactory. Pine that is all sapwood would be able to be treated to H6 but would not have the abrasion resistance needed.

The ideal piece of timber would have the properties of turpentine when it is submerged in the salt water and above the water. Where the CityCats rub they would have the properties of spotted gum. Unfortunately, such a timber does not exist, but can it be created? Theoretically yes. By incising a spotted gum rubbing strip to a depth of 20mm and treating first with CCA and then pigment emulsified creosote (PEC), a piece of timber with H6 properties is created, i.e. equal to turpentine. In practice the answer is "No". The sides are tapered so they cannot be incised. Further, the abrasion from the CityCats would soon wear away the H6 treatment. The reality is also that the Australian hardwoods are so hard that it is probably not possible to incise to the correct depth.

So, we have a situation where neither natural durability nor treatment nor a combination of the two will provide an answer. I would suggest that an answer might be
- Use thicker timber so the time between changes is extended
- Use old tech turpentine piles for the skewing piles.

H5 (CCA) Applications in Playgrounds

Figure 65. These playground posts cannot be H5 with CCA. (H5 in ACQ was not readily available.

When a specifier asks for H5, in practice it can only be met in hardwood and pine in Queensland with CCA. What client is going to accept CCA these days for human contact? (Treatment to H5 with the alternatives is theoretically possible but not easily commercially available). This is an even greater problem when the posts are part of a children's playground. Sometimes it is necessary to do a "work around". The playground illustrated has handrail posts that go into the ground, a H5 (CCA) application which is not permitted. Our "work around" was to use Durability 1 In Ground timber and measured the required diameter under the sapwood i.e. a 200mm post became a 225mm post. The sapwood was treated to H3 with Tanalith E. The sapwood above ground will not degrade over its life span. Most likely, the sapwood in the ground will remain intact also but it does not matter if it does not.

Untreated Hoop Pine Chamfers

Figure 66.   Untreated Hoop after 100 years.

Figure 67.   Untreated Slash pine after 15 years.

If we take AS5604-2005 as our guide we would expect an untreated hoop pine (Durability Class 4 Above Ground) chamfer board to last a maximum of eight years.[244] Yet against the odds there are thousands of homes in Queensland clad in untreated hoop pine where the original boards are over 100 years old? Can we expect that lifespan today? The short answer is "No".

In about 1992 I processed some untreated slash pine at a customer's direction into cladding. I advised against doing this, but the builder's argument was that as there were all these untreated hoop pine clad buildings that are performing very well so his must also. Foolishly I complied with his request. Initially, with a clear gloss over the pine the building looked great I have to admit, but, in about 15 years. The cladding started to decay badly where there was shade. After almost 20 years there are patches of decay over all the weather exposed walls. What has changed over the intervening 100 years?

Two factors have changed:
- The old hoop was from virgin forest and of higher quality and presumably more dense and with less sapwood; and,
- The detailing of old structures was generally done to higher standard – e.g. bigger overhangs, verandas.

Performance of 100 years ago is no guarantee of an equivalent performance with modern fast-grown plantation softwood timbers. Preservation in conjunction with successful old design practices (and they were not all successful) are required with today's plantation pines.

---

[244] Table 1.

Change in Hazard Level Over Time

The timber in the treated pine trussed bridge illustrated is presumably treated to H3. After the soil has encroached on it (and really in any case where there is less than about 200mm clearance), it has changed from being a H3 to a H5 application. The Timberlife design life prediction software estimates the serviceability (50 % strength) of a 150x50 treated to H3 when used in an above ground application of somewhere between 75 to 90 years and replacement at about 100 years. When the same timber is in ground contact it only has a serviceability of 25 years!

Figure 68.   No side walls allow soil to encroach on H3 treated timber

I am not aware of a structural H5 incised pine that could be used in the bottom cord of this truss. This example shows that careful thought has to be given to design to ensure that the hazard level on the day of construction is the hazard level that can be expected over the extended service life. This bridge should have terminated with a concrete abutment incorporating sidewalls with the timber spaced at least 50mm above the abutment.

CONCLUSION

Over many years, I have had to work through the frustrating complications caused by over-specification of timber treatment such as asking for H5 (CCA) or H6 (CCA and PEC) for applications which are only H3. The lower H ratings can be easily met with new generation non-chrome, non-arsenic treatments, whereas, with sawn timber, the higher ratings are often impossible to meet and always have been impossible to meet in a meaningful sense. In conjunction with over specification of treatment would often be poor specification (if at all) of natural durability and poor building practices. This Guide to timber preservation has hopefully highlighted that, in reality, for anything above H3, it is probably not going to happen on sawn timber. Success will be dependent on a correct specification of natural durability and good building practices in conjunction with an appropriate level of timber treatment.

SOURCE OF IMAGES

Cover	Treatment plant	Arch Timber Protection U.K.
Figure 4	Empty sapwood vessels	Gary Hopewell, DAF
Figure 5	Plugged heartwood vessels	Gary Hopewell, DAF
Figure 6	Prefinished components	Mark Iley/LOSP Reference Library
Figure 8	Aerosol end sealants	Lonza Wood Protection
Figure 11	Creosote treated fencing	Gunns Agricultural, Kalangadoo.
Figure 12	Extreme degrade at groundline	Energex
Figure 14	Soft rot at groundline	Laurie Cookson of CSIRO
Figure 19	Lyctus attack	Trevor Smith, South Coast Home Check
Figure 20	Lyctus Larvae	Doug Howick
Figure 24	Matthew Powell	Incised post installed upside down
Figure 27	Graveyard Trails	Jack Norton, DPI Forestry
Figure 28	End Attack of Pile offcut	Arch Wood Protection (Aust) Pty Limited
Figure 31	Untreated marine piles	Bligh Tanner Consulting Engineers
Figure 32	Encased iron bark	Bligh Tanner Consulting Engineers
Figure 36	Sons of Gwalia	Greg Meachem
Figure 37	Corrosion hazard	Forest and Wood Products Australia
Figure 39	Old galvanised bolts	Timber Queensland
Figure 41	Z275 bracket	Multinail
Figure 42	Test structure	BRANZ
Figure 43	Corrosion rates	BRANZ
Figure 44	Painted Bolts	ITW Proline
0	Colour coded framing	Hyne
0	Cylindrical Auger beetle	Doug Howick
0	Cartoon	Fiona Robbe
0	Leaching trials	Arch Wood Protection (Aust) Pty Limited
0	Contact trials	Arch Wood Protection (Aust) Pty Limited
0	Playground Posts	Contrast Constructions
All other images are from the author		

REFERENCES

Anonymous. "Fastener Durability in Timber", *Corrosion Management,* Industrial Galvanisers, Ed. John Robinson, (May 2005).

Anonymous. *Preservative Treated Wood Technical Bulletin No. T-PRWOOD08-R* (Pleasanton: Simpson Strong-Tie, 2008),

APVMA. *The Reconsideration of Registrations of Arsenic Timber Treatment Products (CCA and arsenic trioxide) and Their Associated Labels - Report Of Review Findings And Regulatory Outcomes Final Report Part 1 - Toxicological Assessment* (Canberra, 2005). URL: http://www.apvma.gov.au/products/review/docs/arsenic_tox.pdf. Date accessed, April 22, 2012

Arch Wood Protection (Aust) Pty Ltd. *Tanalised Outdoor Wood Guarantee, January 2012*

Arch Wood Protection (SA) Pty Ltd. *Guaranteed Peace of Mind*: URL: http://www.archchemicals.com/Fed/WOODSA/Docs/Guarantee_Brochure.pdf Date Accessed, January 14, 2012.

Arch Wood Protection, Inc. and Arch Treatment Technologies, Inc Hardware Recommendations for Treated Wood June 6, 2006: URL: http://www.archchemicals.com/Fed/WOLW/Docs/corrosiontechnote.pdf Date accessed, 12 February 2012.

Australian Government. *Approved Timber Permanent Preservative Formulations.* URL: https://www.agriculture.gov.au/import/goods/timber/approved-treatments-timber/permanent-preservative-treatment/approved-timber-permanent-preservative-formulations Date accessed: September 19, 2020.

Bagley, S.T. and D.L. Richter. *Biodegradation of Brown Rot Fungi in The Mycota, A Comprehensive Treatise on Fungi as Experimental Systems for Basic and Applied Research Vol 10 Industrial Applications*. Ed. By Karl Esser, Joan W. Bennett, H. D. Osiewacz. (Berlin: Springer-Verlaq, 2002).

Bluescope Steel. *Corrosion, Contact With Timber Technical Bulletin CTB-13* Rev 4, 2008.

Bootle, Keith R. *Wood in Australia, Types, properties and uses, Second Edition*. (North Ryde: McGraw Hill Australia, 2005).

Branz. *Timber Treatment*. URL: https://www.weathertight.org.nz/new-buildings/timber-treatment/ Date Accessed: September 20, 2020.

Cambpell-McFarlane, Jacqueline. *Creosote and its Use as a Wood Preservative*. U.S. Environment Protection Agency URL: http://www.epa.gov/pesticides/factsheets/chemicals/creosote_main.htm Date accessed, April 10, 2012

Carter Holt Harvey. *Garden Walls*. URL: http://www.chhwoodproducts.com.au/userfiles/6/file/

CHH075%20Garden%20Walls%20A5-v1.pdf Date accessed, 11 December 2010.

Carter Holt Harvey. *Ironwood Landscaping* URL: http://www.chhwoodproducts.com.au/ironwoodlandscaping/. Date accessed, 11 December 2010.

Cookson L, M Hedley. *Adequacy of H3 LOSP tin based preservative treatment for exposed external structural uses.* (Melbourne: Australian Government, 2005).

CRC Industries (Aust) Pty. Limited. *Technical Data Sheet Product No. 3013,3014, 3015,3016.*

CSIRO. The Facts about CCA treated timber Page 7. URL: http://www.csiro.au/en/Outcomes/Food-and-Agriculture/CCATreatedTimber/CCA-safety-overview.aspx. Date accessed, 21 April 2012.

Ebsworth H.W.L. *Australian Consumer Law – Summary of Changes* January 2011. URL: http://www.hwlebsworth.com.au/files/TP.pdf. Date Accessed, 12 January 2012.

Davis, Robin I. revised Jack Norton *Corrosion of Metal in Contact with Wood* Queensland Forest Research Institute Timber Note 2, Revised August 1988.

Davis, Robin I. *Timber Preservatives and Corrosion,* International Research Group on Wood Preservation, Working Group III, Preservatives and Method of Treatment (Document IRG/WP/3228). Prepared for the 14th annual meeting Gold Coast, 1983.

Frame and Truss Manufacturers Association of Australia. *Timber Treatment Compliance, Fabricators must do Due Diligence.* No publication details.

Francis, L.P., J. Norton, *Above-Ground Durability Estimation in Australia, Results after 16 Years Exposure,* International Research Group on Wood Protection, IRG/WP 05-20314. 2005.

Friday Offcuts. *Kop-coat Launches Proceedings Against Competitor.* (September 13, 2103) URL: https://fridayoffcuts.com/dsp_article.cfm?id=544&aid=5834 Date Accessed: September 16, 2020.

Greaves, H and K.J. McCarthy *Inspection and Maintenance Procedures for Ground-Line Defects in Wood Poles* in Proceedings of the ESAA Pole Symposium, Gold Coast, 1980.

Greaves, Harry. *Environmental Aspects of Wood Preservation.* 22nd Forest Products Research Conference, 1986.

Greaves, Harry. *Current Trends in Protection of Timber.* 13th All Australia Timber Congress Nov 1990.

Greaves, Harry. *Pigment Emulsified Creosote (PEC) - Improved Oil-based Preservatives* in Ann. Rev. Div. Chem. & Wood Technol. (CSIRO, 1986).

Gunns Timber Products. *Treated Pine Kiln Dried.* URL: http://www.gunnstimber.com.au/products/pine/treatedPineKilnDried/index.php. Date accessed, 11 December 2010.

Hyne. Hyne T2 Red. URL: http://www.hyne.com.au/t2red/index.html. Date accessed, 15 May 2011.

Hyne. Hyne T2 Blue. URL: http://www.hyne.com.au/our_business/hynet2blue.html. Date accessed, 15 May 2011.

Hyne. Hyne T3 Green. URLhttp://www.hyne.com.au/our_business/hynet3green.html. Date accessed, 15 May 2011.

Kear, G. M.S. Jones, P.W. Haberecht. *Corrosion of Mild steel HDG Steel and 316 Stainless Steel in CCA CuAz and ACQ treated Pinus Radiata.* Corrosion and Prevention Conference of the Australasian Corrosion Association Inc, Gold Coast, 2005. Paper 064.

Kear, G, Hai-Zhen Wu, Mark Jones . The *Corrosion of Metallic Fasteners in Untreated, CCA-, CuAz-, and ACQ-based timbers. Branz Study Report* 153. (Judgeford: Branz, 2006).

Koppers Wood Products Pty. Ltd. *Treated Hardwood Marine Piles Case Studies* Revision 0, 2009.

Koppers Wood Products Pty. Ltd. *Treated Hardwood Foundation Piles* - Case Studies Revision 0, 2009.

Koppers performance Chemicals. *Wood Product Warranty 2016.* URL: http://www.kopperspc.com.au/pdfs/koppers-wood-product-warranty.pdf. Date accessed: October 5, 2020.

Lebow, Stan. *Fixation of CCA.* (Granbury: American Wood Preservers Association. 1998). This document is attached to the proceedings of the Ninety-Sixth Annual Meeting of the American Wood-Preservers' Association San Francisco, 2000, Volume 96.

Leightley, L.E. *Technical and Operational Aspects and In-Service Performance of Preservative Treated Poles* in Proceedings of the ESAA Pole Symposium, Gold Coast, 1980.

Li, Z.W., N.J. Marston and M.S. Jones. *Corrosion of Fasteners in Treated Timber* (Study Report SR241 2011) Branz, 2011.

Li. Cuoxin, Shanjing Xia, Yilang Peng. Anti-Corrosion Performance of Four Hot Dip Galvanising Bolts in *Applied Mechanics and Materials Vols. 395-396* (2013).

Lonza. *Azotek, Glueline based protection for LVL and I-Beams against insects and decay.* (Otahuhu: Lonza, 2017).

Lonza. *Permatek, Solutions for the control of insects in engineered Wood Products.* (Otahuhu: Lonza, 2017).

Mai, C. and Militz H. *Chemical Wood Protection in Wood Production, Wood Technology, and Biotechnological Impacts.* Kues, Ursula (Ed). (Universitatsverlag Gottingen, 2007).

Nguyen, Minh N., Robert H. Leicester, and Chi-hsiang Wang. *Manual 6 – Embedded corrosion of fasteners in exposed timber structures*. (Melbourne. Forest and Wood Products Australia: 2007.

Nguyen, Minh N., Robert H. Leicester, and Chi-hsiang Wang. *Manual 7 – Marine borer attack on timber structures*. (Melbourne: FWPA. 2008).

Osmose. *Naturwood ACQ*. 2006.

Osmose. *Lifewood CCA*. 2006.

Pryda. *Technical Update - Corrosion resistance of Pryda products*. Feb. 2012.

Pryda. *Technical Update - Corrosion resistance of trusses over enclosed swimming pools*. March, 2009.

Queensland Government. *Timber Utilisation and Marketing Act* (Queensland Government Printer, 1987).

Rammer, Douglas, Samuel Zelinka, Philip Line. *Fastener Corrosion: Testing, Research and Design Considerations*, a paper given at World Conference on Timber Engineering 2006.

Read, Deborah. *Report on Copper Chrome and Arsenic Treated Timber*. ERMANZ April 2003 URL: http://archive.ermanz.govt.nz/resources/publications/ pdfs/cca-report.pdf. Date accessed, 21 April 2012

Riverland Treated Pine. URL: http://www.riverlandtreatedpine.com.au/FAQ.html. Date accessed, 11 December 2010.

Robinson, John. *Specifiers Manual*. (Carole Park: Industrial Galvanisers, 2013).

Solver Paints *L.O.S.P. Treated Pre Primed Timber SS-127* January 2008. URL: http://solverpaints.com.au/documents/msds-pdf/10-SECTION%20SS%20%20(Specifications%20&%20Surface%20Prep.)/SS-127.pdf Date accessed, 30 January 2012.

Timber Preservers Association of Australia *Fasteners in CCA Treated Timber*. URL http://www.tpaa.com.au/fastenerscca.htm Date accessed, 25 March 2012.

Timber Queensland. *Technical Data Sheet 22, Light Organic Solvent Preservative Treated Timber*. March 2014.

Vicbeam. *Vic ash H3 Hardwood*. URL: https://vicbeam.com.au/product-services/gl18-vic-ash-h3-hardwood/ Date accessed: September 16, 2020.

Wallis, Norman K. *Australian Timber Handbook*. (Sydney: Angus and Robinson, 1956).

Wilkinson, J.G. *Industrial Timber Preservation*. (London: Associated Business Press, 1979).

Zelinka, Samuel. Corrosion of Metals in Wood Products in Developments in *Corrosion Protection*. (InTech, 2014).

Zelinka, Samuel, Rebecca Sichel, Donald Stone. Exposure testing of fasteners in preservative treated wood: Galvimetric corrosion rates and corrosion product analysis in *Corrosion Science* 52 (2010).

ABOUT THE AUTHOR

Ted's family had been involved in sawmilling and building for about 140 years and a lot of knowledge has passed through the generations. In 1985 he ventured into the footbridge market (almost by accident) and then followed public landscaping. Initially he just did as he was told by consultants who knew very little about timber. In about 1988 Ted decided he would come to know the medium he was working with far better than any of his competitors and most of the professionals who used his products.

Through years of reading, observation and formal research projects undertaken on his behalf by Australia's leading specialist engineers and designers he was able to develop products with the expertise to match. There was no one in Australia who could match him in when it came to weather exposed timber. In his semi-retirement he works as a consultant in this field and is writing down what he has learnt over a lifetime, so it does not have to be relearnt.